D1164994

Diocese
of Immigrants:
THE BROOKLYN
CATHOLIC EXPERIENCE

1853-2003

COAT OF ARMS
(Appearing on Title Page)
DIOCESE OF BROOKLYN

In the Diocesan coat of arms, the shield is divided by a golden cross which represents the Catholic faith. It has been planted in the Counties of Kings and Queens, as expressed by the two crowns. The roundles with wavy silver and black lines suggest the etymology of the name of Brooklyn. The topography reminded the early Dutch settlers of Breuckelen in Holland. A silver shield in the center bears an escallop shell, the symbol of St. James the Greater, the titular of the Cathedral-Basilica.

Publisher
Éditions du Signe
B.P. 94
67038 Strasbourg cedex 2
France
Tel: 011 33 3 88 78 91 91
Fax: 011 33 3 88 78 91 99
Email: info@editionsdusigne.fr

Publishing Director
Christian Riehl

Director of Publication
Joëlle Bernhard

Publishing Assistant
Audrey Gilger

Design and Layout
Daniel Muller - M@W

Photoengraving
Editions du Signe - 105454

Copyright Text
© The Diocese of Brooklyn, 2004

Copyright Design and Layout
© Éditions du Signe, 2004
All Rights reserved
Reproduction forbidden

ISBN 2-7468-0912-5

Printed in Italy by Canale

My Dear Brothers and Sisters in Christ,

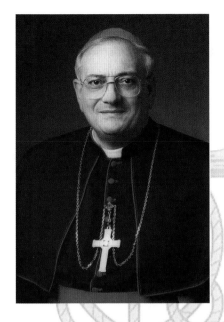

O n October 3, 2003, in the homily at my Mass of Installation as the Seventh Bishop of the Diocese of Brooklyn, I reflected on the image of the Church as a family. Historically, the Church in Brooklyn has developed as a family of immigrants representing people from all over the world. The old and new immigrants alike came, and continue to come, to live in freedom, to work, to raise a family, and to practice their faith.

Diocese of Immigrants: the Brooklyn Catholic Experience, 1853-2003 traces the highlights of our diocesan history. My predecessor, Bishop Thomas V. Daily, commissioned this work to serve as a reminder of the extraordinary witness of faith which has been found in the bishops, clergy, men and women in consecrated life, and lay faithful who have been building a cathedral of "living stones" (1 Peter 2:5) for more than one hundred and fifty years. This text completes the 2003 Diocesan Sesquicentennial celebrations.

Diocese of Immigrants: the Brooklyn Catholic Experience, 1853-2003, in its narrative and its use of images, invites us to reflect on our unique historic pilgrimage as a "diocese of immigrants." As one travels throughout our country, we often meet people who lived for a time within the boundaries of the Diocese of Brooklyn. Their memories are also a vital part of our diocesan legacy. Mr. Joseph Coen, Dr. Patrick McNamara, and Fr. Peter Vaccari have provided a glimpse into the history of our diocesan pilgrimage of faith and love.

It is my hope and prayer that we can draw on the lessons of the past. The stories of heroic, sacrificial love and service to the local community have been expressions of a vibrant faith that has not been afraid to venture into unexplored waters. At the dawn of the new millennium, we entrust ourselves to Mary, the Mother of the Church. She always leads us to her Son, Jesus. In Him and in His Body, the Church, we once again "put out into the deep" as we accept the challenges of the 21st Century.

May our appreciation for the past, and our steadfast commitment to the present, enable us to become beacons of hope in the future as we seek "to be the Church on pilgrimage, making our way to the kingdom of God" (from the Homily at the Mass of Installation).

Sincerely in Christ,

Nicholas di Marzio

Most Reverend Nicholas DiMarzio, Ph.D., D.D.
Bishop of Brooklyn

GUIDE TO THE IMAGES ON THE BOOK COVER

Front Cover (From left to right, top to bottom):

• Bishop Thomas V. Daily visits the Diocese's Chinese community, 1997.
• The Mangano brothers at St. Finbar, Bath Beach, 1963.
• Archbishop McEntegart celebrates his golden jubilee of ordination at St. James Cathedral, 1967.
• Sister Marie André reminds her students that February is Catholic Press Month, 1960.
• Pope John Paul II greets Bishop Mugavero in Rome, 1983.
• Msgr. Archibald V. McLees receives a flag from the local Catholic War Veterans Chapter, 1963.
• St. Stanislaus Kostka students celebrate the parish centennial, 1996.
• Angel Guardian Home in the early 1960's.
• Puerto Rican Catholics celebrate *La Fiesta de Nuestra Señora de Providencia* at St. Brigid, Wyckoff Heights, 1997.
• Bishop Fulton J. Sheen visits St. John's Preparatory School, Bedford-Stuyvesant, 1965.
• Mexican Catholics celebrate *La Fiesta de Nuestra Señora de Guadalupe* at Guardian Angel, Brighton Beach, 1997.
• Croatian Catholics participate in a multi-ethnic Mass at St. James Cathedral-Basilica, 1993.
• Italian Eucharistic Congress, Bensonhurst, 1961.
• Good Friday procession at St. Pancras, Glendale, during the 1970's.
• Cathedral Preparatory Seminary, Elmhurst, 1981.
• Ghanaian Catholics outside Our Lady of Lourdes, Queens Village, 1990's.
• Bishop John Loughlin dedicates the Cathedral of the Immaculate Conception, Fort Greene, June 1868.
• The Mazzucco family outside St. Paul, Cobble Hill (now St. Peter-St. Paul-Our Lady of Pilar), 1965.
• Bishop Thomas E. Molloy after his consecration as an Auxiliary Bishop, 1920.
• Parish play at St. Thomas More-St. Edmund, Breezy Point.
• Father John Powis speaks at a rally for the Nehemiah Project, Brownsville, 1982.
• Adult baptism at Christ the King parish, Springfield Gardens.
• Bishop Charles E. McDonnell (seated, center) with priests and seminarians, 1912.
• Bishop Nicholas DiMarzio with the Auxiliary Bishops of the Diocese, October 2003.
• Our Lady Queen of Martyrs Swim Team in the 1970's.
• Sixth grade boys, St. Cecelia, Greenpoint, 1962.

Back Cover (From left to right, top to bottom):

• Bishop Kearney High School, Bensonhurst, 1961.
• NYPD bag pipers at the Bay Ridge St. Patrick's Day Parade, 1997.
• Memorial Day Service, Holy Child Jesus, Richmond Hill, 1927.
• Diocesan Eucharistic Rally at Arthur Ashe Stadium, Flushing, June 2000.
• CCD class at St. James Cathedral, 1968.
• Catholic Charities celebrates its centennial at Brooklyn's Borough Hall, 1999.
• Mother De Chantal Keating, C.S.J., at St. John's Home for Boys, Bedford-Stuyvesant, ca. 1890.
• Ordination Class, St. James Cathedral-Basilica, 1997.
• Archbishop Molloy High School Track Team, ca. 1960.
• Bishop Thomas V. Daily with Knights of Columbus Honor Guard outside Our Lady of Perpetual Help Basilica, Bay Ridge, 1995.
• Mission Sunday, St. Michael, Flushing, in the late 1950's.
• La Sociedad del Santo Nombre, Our Lady of Pilar, 1935.
• Corpus Christi procession, St. Jerome, Flatbush, 2000.
• FDNY Chaplain Father John Delendick at Ground Zero, September 2001.
• St. John's Hospital, Long Island City, 1944.
• Sunday School Class, St. Peter Claver, Bedford-Stuyvesant, 1920.
• Diocesan Commission on the Elderly meets at the Immaculate Conception Center, Douglaston, 2001.
• Baseball Team, Sacred Heart, Bayside, 1912.
• Permanent Diaconate ordinations, St. James Cathedral-Basilica, 1998.
• *Tablet* reporter Ed Wilkinson (left), 1973.
• Feast of Our Lady of Mount Carmel, Williamsburg, July 1997.
• Holy Cross School, Flatbush, January 1942.
• Vietnamese Catholics at St. Aloysius, Ridgewood, 1993.
• A Women's Cursillo at St. Paul's Center, in the late 1960's.
• Brooklyn priests who studied at the North American College are ordained in Rome, 1970.
• Byzantine Rite Mass, Sacred Heart Convent, Astoria, 1963.

TABLE OF CONTENTS

This stained glass window is
from St. James Cathedral-
Basilica (1822).

CHAPTER ONE

Long Island and Brooklyn in the Pre-Diocesan Era
(1524-1853)

When the Florentine explorer Giovanni da Verrazano discovered New York Bay in 1524, he became the first European to visit what is now New York State. In the early seventeenth century, the Dutch settled the region and named it New Netherland. Its capital was New Amsterdam (now Manhattan). During the 1630's the Dutch settled western Long Island and founded several towns, among them Flatlands, Flatbush, New Utrecht and Bushwick. In 1646, the Dutch West India Company issued a charter for the town of Breuckelen (Dutch for "broken lane"). Now known as Brooklyn, it was named for a city in Holland. Beginning in 1640, the English settled eastern Long Island, naming their settlements after English towns such as Southold and Southampton.

During the seventeenth century, French Jesuits operating out of Canada planted the seeds of Catholicism in New York. They and their lay associates worked among the Native peoples in what is now upstate New York. One testimony to their success is the life and work of Blessed Kateri Tekakwitha (1656-1680), known as the "Lily of the Mohawks." Missionary work, however, could be dangerous business. Between 1642 and 1649, six Jesuits and two lay missionaries were tortured and murdered by the Iroquois. In 1930, Pope Pius XI canonized them together as the North American Martyrs.

One of these Jesuits, Father Isaac Jogues, had been captured by the Iroquois in 1643. Jogues was released through the help of a Dutch Reformed Minister, John Megapolensis, who brought him to New Amsterdam. Jogues stayed there

7

The Pre-Diocesan Era (1524-1853)

❖ *This statue of St. Isaac Jogues stands outside American Martyrs parish, founded in Bayside in 1948.*

for several weeks before returning to France. In New Amsterdam, he noted the Dutch regime's attempt to impose Calvinism on the people. The New Netherland Charter of 1640 prohibited the practice of any other religion than the Dutch Reformed. The only documentation of public dissent was the 1656 case of "Nicholas the Frenchman" from Breuckelen. Nicholas was cited for refusing to pay a tax for the minister's salary, and "insolently pleaded the frivolous excuse... that he was a Catholic." New Amsterdam's population consisted of Protestant, Jewish, and Catholic settlers (both forced and voluntary) from Africa, continental Europe, the British Isles, and elsewhere. Even then, New York was a multicultural society, an immigrant community.

Catholicism and Anti-Catholicism in Colonial New York

In 1664, the Dutch ceded New Netherland to the English. Renamed New York, it became a proprietorship of James, the Duke of York. (James became a Catholic in 1672.) In 1682 he appointed Colonel Thomas Dongan, an Irishman, as governor. In 1683 Dongan came to New York by way of Long Island, accompanied by his personal chaplain, an English Jesuit named Thomas Harvey. Father Harvey may well have celebrated the first Mass on Long Island. On August 26, 1683, on the site of the old Federal Customs House, he celebrated the first Mass on Manhattan Island. Dongan was a capable administrator and diplomat. On October 30, he called an assembly which enacted the "Charter of Liberties and Privileges." The Charter granted religious freedom to all who professed "faith in God by Jesus Christ."

❖ *The North American Martyrs are depicted in this stained glass window from Our Lady of Fatima, a parish founded in Jackson Heights in 1948.*

The Pre-Diocesan Era (1524-1853)

❖ *Thomas Dongan, the Second Earl of Limerick (1634-1715), was a pioneer of religious freedom in America.*

In 1685, the Duke of York became King James II of England. Religious toleration in New York came to an end in 1688 with England's "Glorious Revolution," which overthrew King James. By then, Dongan had left New York. When news of the revolution reached the colony, Jacob Leisler, a Dutch merchant started a rebellion that overthrew the governor. During the upheaval, the Jesuits fled New York. In 1691, Leisler was forcibly replaced by a royal governor. A new colonial assembly modified Dongan's charter to deny religious freedom in New York "for any person of the Romish religion." By the time of the American Revolution, ten of the thirteen colonies had anti-Catholic laws on the books.

In 1697, Richard Coote, the notoriously anti-Catholic Earl of Bellomont, became Governor of New York. In August 1700, the assembly passed a law subjecting any Catholic priest caught performing any religious ceremony to "perpetual imprisonment." Any colonist who aided or harbored a priest was subject to imprisonment and a £200 fine. In his history of the New York Archdiocese, Msgr. Thomas Shelley writes:

English North America was an overwhelmingly Protestant world in the colonial period, and would remain so well into the era of the new American republic. These Protestant colonists may not have been especially fervent church-goers, and they were themselves divided into rival denominations. Yet there was one common element in their religious beliefs that united them, and that was a detestation of Roman Catholicism, or, as they would have said, "popery."

In 1748, an Anglican minister wrote that there was not "the least face of popery" in New York. Catholic growth during the eighteenth century was slow. For Mass, Catholics had to await the arrival of itinerant priests who traveled throughout the colonies. In such a situation, it was inevitable that laypeople would exercise a spiritual leadership, leading prayer services and Scripture readings. Because of their loyalty to Rome, and because of their historic ties to the French and Spanish, England's traditional enemies, Catholic colonists were inherently suspect in the eyes of their Protestant neighbors. The charge of divided allegiances supplied fuel for an anti-Catholicism that was expressed in cartoons, books, newspapers, and even the pulpit.

Catholics and the American Revolution

Even today, one can see numerous testimonies to the American Revolution throughout Brooklyn. In Fort Greene Park, the Prison Ship Martyrs Monument commemorates the 11,000 patriots who died aboard British prison ships in Wallabout Bay during the wartime occupation of New York. In 1897, a monument was erected in Prospect Park to the "Maryland Four Hundred," a predominantly Catholic regiment that distinguished itself in the Battle of Long Island in 1776. The Old Stone House in Park Slope was the site of a key action during that battle. (It later became the original clubhouse for the Brooklyn Dodgers.)

The revolutionary era was a significant period for American Catholics, who were involved in every aspect of the war effort: diplomatic, political, and military. In 1776 the Continental Congress sent a mission to Montreal that included Benjamin Franklin, Samuel Chase, Charles Carroll (the only Catholic to sign the Declaration of Independence), and his cousin, Father John Carroll. The mission's goal was to enlist Canadian support for the war. Although the mission failed, the participation of two leading Catholics was

The Pre-Diocesan Era (1524-1853)

❖ *The Fort Greene Prison Ship Martyrs Monument, as seen in the nineteenth century.*

❖ *General George Washington leads American troops at the Battle of Long Island, August 1776.*

an important example of Catholic support for the revolution.

Many Catholic colonists served in the Continental Army, while others participated in the debates that led to the formation of the republic. Catholic nations such as Poland, Spain and France, provided military and economic aid. By the end of the war, Catholics, although a small percentage of the total population, had proven their loyalty to the principles that underlay the revolution. Two Catholics signed the United States Constitution, Daniel Carroll and Thomas FitzSimons.

The Revolution had a significant impact on religious freedom in the newly formed republic. In 1777, the New York State Constitution allowed freedom of religion. However, it did require an oath against all foreign allegiances, both ecclesiastical and civil. When Francis Cooper, a Catholic, was elected to the State Assembly in 1806, he refused to take this oath. In response, over 1,300 Catholics from New York

City successfully petitioned for the repeal of the oath, and Cooper took his seat in the Assembly on February 7, 1806.

Catholics in the Early Republic

In June 1784, Father John Carroll was elected "Superior of the Mission in the thirteen United States." In 1789, Pope Pius VI created the Diocese of Baltimore, with Carroll as the first Bishop. His jurisdiction extended over the entire nation. The Church of John Carroll's time, approximately 30,000

The Pre-Diocesan Era (1524-1853)

❖ *This monument in Brooklyn's Prospect Park commemorated the Maryland troops who fought in the Battle of Long Island.*

Catholics, was a minority in a predominantly Protestant nation. In 1808, as the Catholic population grew, Baltimore was raised to the status of an archdiocese (and Carroll to Archbishop), and new dioceses were erected in New York, Boston, Philadelphia and Bardstown, Kentucky.

One of Archbishop Carroll's great achievements was to show the American people that Catholicism and democracy were not incompatible. In his writings and his speeches, he stressed the commonalities that all Christians shared. Generally speaking, during the period of the early republic, Protestant-Catholic relations were quite cordial. In 1826, for example,

Bishop John England of Charleston addressed the U.S. Congress on the compatibility between the Church and the U.S. Constitution. Before large numbers of Irish Catholic immigrants came to the country in the 1840's, the American Church was a largely Anglo-American and French entity. By the 1860's, however, Irish leadership would be predominant.

After the various anti-Catholic colonial laws were repealed, it became possible for Catholics to band together and worship publicly. Because priests were few, laypeople were often forced to assume the task of actually founding the parish. In the absence of a resident pastor, they formed boards of trustees to administer parishes. New York State's first Catholic parish, St. Peter's on Barclay Street in Manhattan, was founded in 1785. Its early years were difficult ones. Conflicts arose among the priests, between the priests and the trustees, and even between the trustees and Bishop Carroll himself.

❖ *Archbishop John Carroll (1735-1815), the first Roman Catholic Bishop in the United States.*

❖ *A Brooklyn road, as seen in 1776.*

From 1785 to 1855, historian Patrick Carey writes, the movement known as "trusteeism" was a significant force in American Catholic life, the underdeveloped state of which required a strong lay initiative. Trustees wanted to elect their own representatives and to participate in the selection (and, if necessary, the removal) of pastors. Many of them felt they were adapting European Catholicism to the American scene, where Congregationalism was the order of the day. Trustees saw laity and clergy as having diffferent ministries, with the laity running temporal affairs and the clergy spiritual. Conflict emerged, however, and internecine battles replaced the original ideal of collaboration.

Trusteeism illustrates an important point about the nature of American Catholic life. One of the guiding principles of American Catholicism has been volunteerism. Whereas the Church in Europe frequently enjoyed the financial support of the state,

Catholicism in the United States depended on the freely given financial support and volunteer work of the laity. American Catholics were forced to pool their resources, to collaborate, and to develop a broad sense of stewardship if the Church were to grow and flourish. In the long run, this served to strengthen the bonds between clergy and laity, thereby giving birth to the great achievements of the Church in America.

The Rise of Brooklyn

New York City was the nation's capital from 1789 to 1790. Over the next century, its commercial and political importance would grow dramatically. On Long Island, the original Dutch settlements such as Flatbush and Bushwick experienced dramatic

❖ *St. Peter's Church on Barclay Street was founded in 1785. It stands across the street from the former site of the World Trade Center.*

population increases. Brooklyn's growth was the most rapid. Important factors here were the establishment of the Brooklyn Navy Yard in 1801, and the introduction of ferry service between Manhattan and Brooklyn in 1814. Brooklyn would soon become a valuable commuter station, and more New Yorkers moved out of overcrowded lower Manhattan.

In 1816, the town of Brooklyn was incorporated as a village. By 1825, its population was nearly 11,000, making it the state's third largest municipality. Brooklyn soon became known as the "capital of Long Island," and it continued to grow throughout the nineteenth century. In 1834, it received its Charter as a city. By 1855, it was the nation's third largest city. In 1898, Brooklyn, Queens, Staten Island and the Bronx were absorbed into the City of New York.

Brooklyn may have lost its independence, but not its unique identity.

The Long Island Rail Road was incorporated in 1834, and would soon be an important supplement to other forms of transportation. By 1837, railroad tracks had reached Hicksville. By 1844, they reached Greenport. The railroad would play an important part in transforming the social as well as the geographical landscape of Long Island. In Queens, the major towns were Jamaica, Flushing and Newtown, which were principally farmlands that afforded easy access to the larger urban centers. Suffolk County's economy centered on farming, fishing and the whaling industry. (Present-day Nassau County was formed out of Queens and Suffolk Counties in 1898.)

❖ *The Old Bushwick Church, as seen in 1828.*

❖ *Seen here is the ferry between New York and Brooklyn.*

❖ *Gowanus Bay, Brooklyn, as seen in the 1840's.*

St. James: The Birth of a Catholic Community

By the early 1800's, immigrants were coming to Long Island in larger numbers. Many of them were Irish and Catholic. Before the Navy Yard was founded, Brooklyn's Catholic population was miniscule. A significant portion of them worked at the Navy Yard. One of them was Peter Turner (1787-1862), who emigrated from County Wexford in his teens and settled on Fulton Street. An Irish neighborhood known as Vinegar Hill, named for a battle fought during the Irish Rebellion of 1798, soon formed near the Navy Yard.

For Mass, Brooklyn Catholics had to take the Fulton Street Ferry to Manhattan, where they attended St. Peter's on Barclay Street. Tradition has it that Brooklyn's first Mass took place in 1820 at William Purcell's home on the corner of York and Gold Streets. It was celebrated by Father Philip Laricy, an Irish-born Augustinian priest. As Catholic numbers increased, Brooklyn Catholics started to talk seriously about getting their own church. On January 1, 1822, Peter Turner sent out a petition to his fellow Brooklyn Catholics:

Whatever we do in word or in work, let us do all in the name of the Lord Jesus Christ: giving thanks to God the father through him. Therefore, in the name of the Lord, – and with the advice and consent of the Right Reverend Bishop, Let the Catholics of Brooklyn having common interests to pursue, and wants to relieve, establish an Association the Better to attain these desirable objects. In the first place, we want our children instructed in the principles of our Holy Religion, we want more convenience

The Pre-Diocesan Era (1524-1853)

❖ *A map of Brooklyn Village, 1816.*

❖ *Jamaica, Queens, as seen in the 1820's.*

❖ *Seen here is an early Long Island Rail Road car.*

in hearing the word of God ourselves. In fact we want a Church, a Pastor, and a place for Interment: all of which with the assistance of Divine Providence, we have every reason to expect by forming ourselves into a well-regulated Society: and as we have not only cheerfully assisted in Building the Churches in this Diocese, from time to time, but nearly all the Churches in the United States lately erected, we have every reason to expect the Cheerful assistance of the Laity, as well as the Right Revd. the Bishop and all his clergy.

Daniel Dempsey's house on Fulton Street served Catholics as a place for business meetings as well as Mass, which was celebrated by priests traveling from Manhattan. Mass was advertised in the *Long Island Star*, a local newspaper. On April 25, 1822, Bishop John Connolly, O.P., the second Bishop of New York, blessed the ground along Chapel and Jay Streets,

where the new church would be built. One reporter described the scene:

April 25, a warm day... In the morning about 11 o'clock I went to see the Roman Catholic Church Yard of the Village (Brooklyn) consecrated – The ceremony was performed by the Rt. Rev. Bishop Connolly and two priests – one of the

FATHER CHARLES CONSTANTINE PISE (1801-1866)

Joy's smiles are not forever,
Nor yet affliction's tears:
Awhile, and I shall never
Feel the weight of years.
The world, when life's brief pageant's o'er,
Shall revel on in joy no more;
But virtue, when my course is run,
Shall waft my soul to Heaven.

"Stream On Ye Tears",
a poem by Father Pise

A novelist, a historian, a poet, and an apologist for the Catholic Church, Charles Constantine Pise was born in 1801 to an Italian father and an American mother in Annapolis, Maryland. After graduating from Georgetown College, he briefly joined the Jesuits before deciding to become a diocesan priest. After studying at Mount Saint Mary's in Emmitsburg, he was ordained a priest in 1825 by Archbishop Ambrose Marechal of Baltimore. While he was still a seminarian, Pise taught at the Mount, where John Hughes, the future Archbishop of New York, was among his students.

After his ordination, Pise served in Baltimore and Washington, D.C., where he soon became renowned as an orator and poet. One of his close friends was Senator Henry Clay of Kentucky, who nominated him for Chaplain to the United States Senate. Pise was the first priest to hold this post (1832-1833), and until recently, the only one.

Father Pise has been called the "founder of Catholic fiction" in America. In 1829, he published a novel, *Father Rowland, a North American Tale*. In addition to novels he wrote history, apologetics, and poetry. In 1834, he went to New York, where he served in several Manhattan parishes. In 1849, he founded St. Charles Borromeo parish in Brooklyn Heights, where he served until his death in 1866. Archbishop John McCloskey of New York presided and preached at the funeral Mass, which was attended by hundreds. A pioneer priest and pastor, Pise was a man of many "firsts."

---

public school system a truly open one, free of discrimination. In New York, however, the fiery Bishop John Hughes, known as "Dagger John," took a more aggressive approach. When faced with the prospect of Nativists burning the city's Catholic churches, he told the Mayor that he would burn ten Protestant churches for every Catholic church that was burned. Over 25 years, Hughes established a network of Catholic churches, schools, convents, hospitals and orphanages that continue to mark the New York landscape.

In 1850, the Diocese of New York became an Archdiocese, and Bishop Hughes an Archbishop. By then New York's Catholic population was growing dramatically. On Long Island, where Catholics had been almost a nonentity in the colonial era, their numbers now reached 15,000. From Greenpoint to Greenport, 23 priests served 22 parishes. By then the Archdiocese had grown too large even for an Archbishop Hughes to handle. Hughes realized that the time had come for a separate diocese on Long Island.

How the Diocese of Brooklyn came to be erected, and the story of its early years, is the subject of the next chapter.

The Pre-Diocesan Era (1524-1853)

❖ Founded in 1841, Our Lady of Mount Carmel, Astoria, was the first Catholic church in Queens County.

❖ St. Patrick, Bay Ridge (1849)

❖ St. Patrick Church was founded on Kent Avenue in Fort Greene in 1843. It was renamed St. Lucy-St.Patrick in 1974.

❖ Archbishop John Hughes (1797-1864)

❖ St. Charles Borromeo, Brooklyn Heights (1849)

❖ St. John the Evangelist, Park Slope (1849)

This statue stands outside St. Teresa, Woodside (1927).

CHAPTER TWO

"A Pioneer Bishop":
Bishop John Loughlin
(1853-1891)

At the First Plenary Council of Baltimore in May 1852, the American bishops gathered to discuss how they could respond more effectively to the growing number of Catholic immigrants. It was here that the erection of the Brooklyn Diocese was first discussed. On May 19, 1852, the bishops wrote to Pope Pius IX, recommending that he establish dioceses in Portland, Burlington, Brooklyn, Newark, Wilmington, Covington, Quincy, Natchitoches, as well as Vicariates Apostolic in Michigan and Florida. At the meeting, Archbishop John Hughes of New York strongly expressed his wish that Father John Loughlin, his Vicar General, be named as Brooklyn's first Bishop.

On July 29, 1853, Pope Pius IX issued the Apostolic Brief, *De Incolumitate Christiani Gregis,* which established the geographical territory of Long Island as its own Diocese, with the episcopal seat in the City of Brooklyn. Father John Loughlin was named Bishop. On September 13, Archbishop Hughes received a copy of the brief. On October 30, 1853, Loughlin was consecrated a bishop, and on November 9, he was installed as Bishop of Brooklyn in St. James Church, which now became St. James Cathedral. At the installation ceremony, Archbishop Hughes declared:

❖ *Born in Brooklyn in 1810, Archbishop John McCloskey of New York became the first American Cardinal in 1875.*

This is a glorious day for the Catholick [sic] Church, for the Church in Brooklyn, for, we may say without any violation of the unity of the Church, that wherever there is a Bishop there is also a Church, not distinct by itself but a member of the Universal Church. Now there is a

❖ *Immaculate Conception of the B.V.M., Williamsburg (1853).*

❖ *Father Joseph Huber with students at St. Fidelis, College Point, 1885.*

Church in Brooklyn where but yesterday there were a few scattered parishes forming a part of the Church of New York. The increase of your numbers, of your zeal... gave rapid proof of the rapid growth of your city and proclaimed that the time had come when Brooklyn needed the care and guidance of a Bishop. So it was recommended in the Council of the assembled Fathers, on a late occasion that this city should be erected into a See and that your present Bishop should be appointed as its ruler. The Holy Father confirmed the recommendation, and you now have a Bishop who comes blessed and consecrated to watch over your spiritual welfare. I know your Bishop long and well. He has for years been the partner of myself in the work of the New York Diocese. He is honored and respected by the clergy and people of New York for his piety and zeal... I predict and look forward to a great increase of piety and the erection of many Churches and schools from the presence and example among you of one in whom the whole American hierarchy have unbounded confidence.

John Loughlin was Bishop of Brooklyn from 1853 to 1891. For both Church and nation, these were years of dramatic change. As the Civil War preserved national unity, westward expansion and industrial growth paved America's road to world power status. Immigration changed the nation from an Anglo-American preserve into a "great American melting

❖ *St. James Cathedral, as seen in 1890.*

Bishop John Loughlin (1853-1891)

❖ Pope Blessed Pius IX (1792-1878)

❖ This stained glass window from St. Teresa of Avila, Sterling Place, depicts Pius IX's proclaiming papal infallibility. Bishop Loughlin is seen to the right.

pot." The American Catholic community grew from a fledgling entity into the nation's largest religious denomination.

The pontificate of Blessed Pius IX (1846-1878) witnessed the end of the Papal States and the declaration of papal infallibility at the First Vatican Council (1869-1870). In 1854, Pius proclaimed the dogma of the Immaculate Conception. His successor Leo XIII (1878-1903) addressed nearly every aspect of modern life in his writings. (He wrote more enyclicals than any other pontiff in history.) In his encyclical *Rerum Novarum* (1891), Leo addressed the injustices that accompanied the rise of industrialism, and he paved the way for modern Catholic social teaching.

On the local scene, Brooklyn became the nation's third largest city. (In 1898 it was incorporated into New York City.) In 1883, the Brooklyn Bridge was completed and the Long Island Rail Road reached Montauk. For the first time, Long Island's population exceeded one million. It was within this context that the Diocese of Brooklyn took shape, under the leadership of a trailblazing Bishop.

Bishop John Loughlin (1853-1891)

❖ *Bishop John Loughlin*

Brooklyn's First Bishop: John Loughlin

John Loughlin was born on December 20, 1817, in County Down, Ireland. As a child his family moved to Albany, New York, where his father opened a grocery business. Loughlin's studies for the priesthood took him from St. Peter's College near Montreal to St. Mary's Seminary in Baltimore. On October 18, 1840, Bishop John Hughes ordained him to the priesthood at Old St. Patrick's Cathedral on Mott Street. Except for four years at St. John's Church in Utica, Loughlin's early priesthood was closely intertwined with the history of Old St. Patrick's Cathedral. (The present Cathedral on Fifth Avenue was begun in 1858 and completed in 1879.)

From the start, Father Loughlin proved himself a capable administrator with a strong pastoral bent. In 1844, Bishop Hughes named Loughlin Rector of the Cathedral, and in 1849 he appointed him Vicar-General of the Diocese. New Yorkers such as Harriett Thompson, an African-American Catholic, noted his strong pastoral bent as he tended to cholera victims during an 1849 epidemic that swept the city. Described as "a smart bustling little man with piercing dark

222   DIOCESS OF BROOKLYN.

DIOCESS OF BROOKLYN.*

This Diocess comprises the whole of Long Island. It is governed by the Rt. Rev. John Loughlin, D. D., who was consecrated on the 30th of October, 1853.

CHURCHES AND CLERGY.

NEW YORK.

St. James' Cathedral, Jay street, residence 188 Jay street—Rt. Rev. John Loughlin, D. D., Rev. Eugene Cassidy, *Rector,* Rev. Samuel A. Mulledy, *Assistant.*

St. Paul's Church, corner of Court and Congress streets—Rev. Joseph A. Schneller, Rev. John Curoe, Rev. Timothy Farrell.

Assumption of B. V. M., corner of York and Jay streets, residence 82 York street—Rev. David W. Bacon, Rev. William Keegan, Rev. P. J. Vieira.

St. Patrick's, Kent Avenue, residence corner of Myrtle Avenue and Ryerson street—Rev. Hugh Maguire

German Church, (not dedicated,) Monroe Avenue—Rev. Maurice Ramsauer.

St. Charles Borromeo, Sidney Place, residence corner of Sidney Place and Livingston street—Rev. Charles C. Pise, D. D.

St. John's, corner of 21st street and 5th Avenue—Rev. Francis McKeon.

St. Joseph's, Pacific street—Rev. Patrick O'Neill.

St. Mary, Star of the Sea, Court street, in progress of erection.

Church, (German,) not dedicated, corner of Willoughby and Bridge streets.

Astoria, Queen's co., B. V. of Mount Carmel—Rev. M. Curran, Rev. Dennis Wheeler.

Babylon, Queen's co.—attended from Jamaica.

Cold Spring, Suffolk co.—attended from Jamaica.

East New York, St. Benedict's—Rev. Maurice Ramsauer.

" " Church in progress—Rev. Andrew Bohan.

Flatbush, King's co., Church of the Holy Cross—Rev. Andrew Bohan.

Flushing, Queen's co., St. Michael's—Rev. James O'Beirne.

Fort Hamilton, St. Patrick's—Rev. Francis McKeon.

Green Port, Suffolk co.—attended from Jamaica.

Jamaica, Queen's co., St. Monica's—Rev. Edward McGinness, Rev. John McCarthy.

James Port—attended occasionally from Jamaica.

Manhasset, Queen's co.—attended once a month from Flushing.

Patchogue, Suffolk co.—attended from Jamaica.

Rockaway, St. Mary's Star of the Sea, every Sunday during the summer months, and occasionally during the remainder of the year.

Sagharbor, St. Andrew's—attended once a month from Jamaica.

Smithtown, Suffolk co.—occasionally from Jamaica.

Westbury, Queen's co., (ch. not dedicated)—occasionally from Jamaica.

*This report was communicated by the Rt. Rev. Bishop.

❖ *The Brooklyn Diocese is listed in the* Catholic Directory *for the first time, 1854.*

eyes," Loughlin was a valued assistant to Bishop Hughes in running a rapidly expanding diocese. It is not difficult to see why Hughes wanted him to be Brooklyn's first Bishop.

During his 38 years as Bishop of Brooklyn, Loughlin more than justified Hughes' confidence in him. Over four decades he oversaw the growth of a Catholic community whose expansion would have been unimaginable to the Reformed Dutch and the English Puritans of an earlier age. In his 1954 history of the Diocese, Monsignor John K. Sharp comments: "He

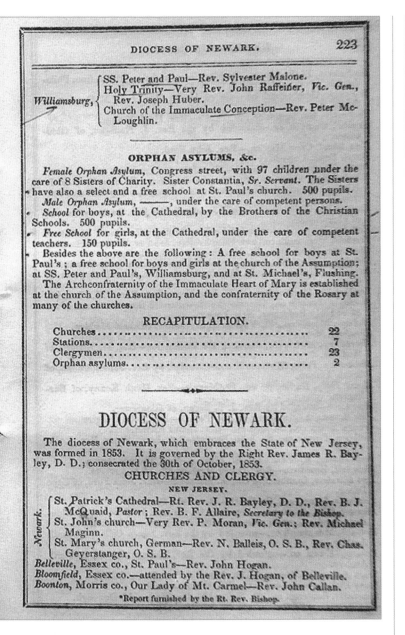

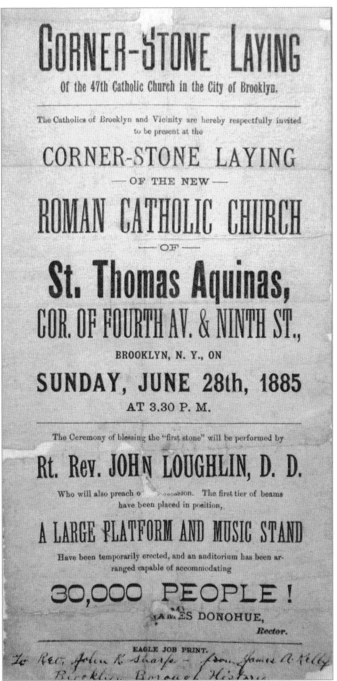

built mightily– churches, schools and institutions." Catholicism was making a big impact on the Brooklyn landscape. In 1872, one newspaper commented:

Year after year develops the progress of Catholicity on Long Island. To the non-Catholic inhabitants of the island, a "Romish Church" is no longer a thing of wonderment, a Roman priest is no longer a stranger. Scarce a village from East New York to Sag Harbor, or from Glen Cove to Rockaway, is without a Church of the grand old faith. Hempstead, erst a village of zealous Protestantism and boasted anti-Romanishness, has now its beautiful cross-crowned Catholic spire, and next Sunday shall have its consecrated altar.

Nativism in Brooklyn

This great success, however, did not come without a price. During its early years, Brooklyn Catholicism had to overcome significant obstacles. Chief among these was the resurgence of Nativism, which reached a fever pitch nationwide in the years preceding the Civil War. As the nation was torn asunder by four years of war, Brooklyn Catholics were not immune to the tragedies of war, either on the battlefield or the home front.

Bishop John Loughlin (1853-1891)

❖ *"The American River Ganges", a political cartoon by Thomas Nast (1871).*

❖ *St. Patrick's Day cartoon, 1867. (Another Nast Cartoon.)*

❖ *St. Malachy, East New York (1854)*

❖ *St. Vincent De Paul, Williamsburg (1860)*

In 1849, a Nativist group calling itself the "Order of the Star Spangled Banner" was formed in New York to oppose the immigrants, specifically Irish Catholic immigrants. They resolved to oppose the growth of Catholic influence in America, especially political. Members of this group took a secret oath; when they were asked about it, they replied, "I know nothing." Hence they became known as the "Know-Nothings."

It is impossible to estimate the exact numbers of the Know-Nothings, although some estimates place their nationwide membership at approximately one million during the 1850's. By then, it was estimated that there were nearly 60 Nativist societies in Brooklyn. A notable Nativist leader in Brooklyn was John S. Orr, known as the "Angel Gabriel" for the flowing robes he wore and the trumpet he blew to warn Brooklyn Protestants about the Roman menace. In May 1854, riots broke out on Atlantic Avenue between Catholics and Nativists, and the mayor of Brooklyn called out troops to restore order. That same year, throughout the nation, the Know-Nothings elected eight governors,

❖ *St. Anthony-St. Alphonsus, Greenpoint (1858)*

Bishop John Loughlin (1853-1891)

❖ *Sunday Mass in the camp of New York's Irish Brigade, 1861.*

over one hundred congressmen, and countless local officials. As the Civil War approached, however, their anti-Catholic platform was overshadowed by larger issues: slavery and the preservation of the Union.

Brooklyn Catholics and the Civil War

On the morning of April 12, 1861, Confederate troops fired on Fort Sumter in Charleston harbor. The Civil War, which would claim the lives of 620,000 Americans North and South, had begun. As President Abraham Lincoln called for volunteers, Catholics on both sides joined in substantial numbers. In Brooklyn, on April 23, nearly 50,000 people attended a war rally in Fort Greene. During the rally, the organizers read a letter from Bishop Loughlin to the crowd:

Dear Sir:
I beg leave to acknowledge the receipt of the invitation with which I am honored to attend the meeting to be held this evening. As it may be impossible for me to be present, I would say that I conceive it to be my duty, as I am admonished, to 'pray for the things that are for peace.'…. The idea of resorting to arms for a settlement between the citizens of our great and glorious country I have endeavored to keep as far as possible from my mind…In whatever circumstances our country may be, we owe loyalty to its constitution and laws and honor to its flag. This I hold to be the duty of every citizen…I shall continue to pray that peace and Union may be restored and permanently established – that the constitution

❖ *St. Michael, East New York (1860)*

❖ *General Thomas W. Sweeney (1820-1892)*

❖ *General Charles P. Stone (1824-1887)*

and laws may be respected and that our flag – the American flag, the flag of the Union, the Star Spangled Banner – may be loved and honored at home and abroad.

MOTHER MARY DE CHANTAL KEATING, C.S.J. (1833 - 1917)

"... I cannot love them too much, for in them I love you. It is your Sacred Body I nurse, whether it be clothed in a soiled blue uniform or a tattered grey. Yours was the human grief I consoled today in the heartbreak of that Confederate mother who wept in my arms."

Mother Mary De Chantal Keating

Jane Constance Keating was born in Tipperary, Ireland, in 1833. She arrived in New York on July 4, 1852. Five years later she became the first postulant to receive the habit of the Sisters of St. Joseph at St. Mary's Convent in Williamsburg. As Sister Mary de Chantal, she served in a variety of capacities: Directress of St. Joseph's Academy in Flushing; Superintendent of the Hospital and Orphanage in Wheeling, West Virginia, during the Civil War; teacher at St. Malachy's Home in East New York; Superior of St. John's Home, Bedford-Stuyvesant, from 1883 until her death 34 years later.

The Archives of the Sisters of St. Joseph in Brentwood, New York, contain the many letters that Mother Keating received from people in all walks of life. These included society ladies, soldiers seeking to understand the meaning of the faith, priests, and the thousands of orphan boys whose lives she guided. Each one sought her prudent

DEATH CALLS MOTHER DE CHANTAL AFTER 60 YEARS AS SISTER OF ST. JOSEPH

One of Pioneer Members of Local Community Had Long Been Head of St. John's Home.

Rev. Mother Mary de Chantal Jane (Keating), one of the first fifteen members of the Sisters of St. Joseph in this borough, died at St. John's Home, Albany and St. Marks avenues, on Monday at noon. Mother de Chantal had been directress of St. John's Home for the past thirty-four years, during which time she had helped mould the character of probably 25,000 boys, many of whom now hold prominent positions throughout the country.

Funeral services for Mother de Chantal were held at the Home Church on Wednesday morning. Mons. John T. Woods celebrated the Mass, with Rev. William Kerwin, as deacon; Rev. Robert O'Donovan, as sub-deacon, and Rev. Walter Kerwin, as master of ceremonies. The eulogy was delivered by Mons. McCarty, who spoke of Mother de Chantal as the exemplification of the ideal religious life. The church was thronged with friends of the deceased Mother. Interment at St. Mary's Cemetery, Flushing, followed the Mass. Members of all the various local Sisterhoods, and scores of priests attended the requiem.

A Notable Career.

Mother de Chantal was born in Kedra, County Tipperary, Ireland, on September 30, 1833. She was fifth in lish Jesuit periodical, *The Month*, and Rev. James Keating, S.J., whose name is well known for his apostolic labors in China and India; her sister, Mother M. Magdalen Keating, foundress of the Presentation Order in Fitchburg, Mass., and two nieces, Mrs. James Ryan, of

MOTHER DE CHANTAL.

guidance and spiritual counsel, which was the fruit of her deeply contemplative prayer in the midst of an energetic and active life of service.

From Williamsburg to Sag Harbor, Catholics responded to Lincoln's call. Many of Most Holy Trinity's parishioners joined the "Schwarze Jaeger," a German-American unit. There were many Brooklynites in Colonel Michael Corcoran's 69th New York, the "Fighting Sixty-ninth," a part of the famed Irish Brigade. A large portion of the Sixth New York Cavalry was made up of men from St. John the Evangelist parish. One Catholic Brooklynite, Sergeant Samuel Graham of the 158th New York, was awarded the Congressional Medal of Honor for bravery. Catholics also helped the war effort in the Brooklyn Navy Yard and in Greenpoint's iron-making factories. Two Union generals had close ties to the Diocese. After the war, General Thomas Sweeney lived in Astoria. In 1892, his funeral Mass was held at Our Lady of Mount Carmel parish. General Charles P. Stone was a convert who lived for many years in Flushing. After the war he became a general in the Egyptian army.

Nearly 600 women religious served on both sides of the war. On the front lines and in the hospitals, sisters ministered to the wounded and the dying. One

Bishop John Loughlin (1853-1891)

❖ *Grand Army Plaza, Brooklyn.*

❖ *Annunciation of the B.V.M., Williamsburg. Founded as as a German parish in 1863, by World War I, it was a center of Lithuanian Catholic life.*

❖ *St. John the Baptist, Bedford-Stuyvesant (1868)*

Brooklyn Josephite, Mother Mary de Chantal Keating, became superintendent of a hospital in Wheeling, West Virginia, where she ministered to Union and Confederate soldiers. Her grave at Mount St. Mary Cemetery, Flushing, is somewhat unique in that it has two headstones. One was placed there by her religious community. The second, erected by the U.S. government, reads: "Comrade to Nurses."

On January 1, 1863, Abraham Lincoln signed the Emancipation Proclamation abolishing slavery. For many years, Brooklyn clergy, Black and white, had taken a leading role in the antislavery movement. Catholic opinion on this issue was never unanimous. Father Sylvester Malone, Pastor of SS. Peter and Paul in Williamsburg, was one of the leading Catholic abolitionists in the New York area. Although Brooklyn's first Black Catholic parish was not established until 1920, there was an African-American presence in Brooklyn's Catholic churches from the start. At St. James Cathedral, for example, the parish sacramental records show that Black parishioners worshipped there as early as the 1830's. In the wake of President Lincoln's assassination on April 14, 1865, Bishop Loughlin expressed his regret for the nation's loss in an open letter to the priests of the Diocese.

The Immigrant Experience

Throughout the war years, immigrants continued to enter the port of New York. Before Ellis Island became the immigration processing center in 1892, immigrants entered the country through Castle Garden in lower Manhattan. The drama of their pilgrimage cannot be understated. Many died on the journey, while the survivors suffered greatly. Many of their children arrived as orphans. At the end of the trip, they encountered a foreign language, a strange culture, and a new political system. Catholic immigrants from continental Europe were coming to a country whose heritage and composition was largely English Protestant, a society that did not entirely welcome them with open arms.

Anna Heck was one of many German immigrants who came to the Williamsburg section of Brooklyn

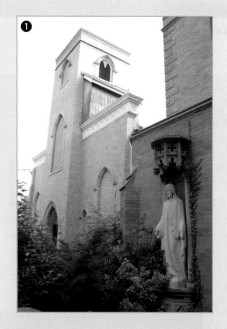

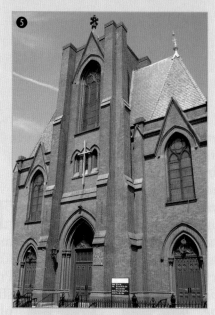

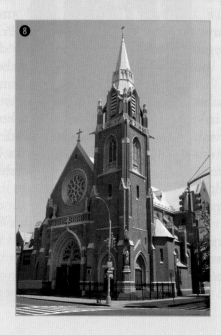

BROOKLYN'S GERMAN PARISHES

Bishop Loughlin founded 18 parishes for German Catholics in Brooklyn and Queens. Seen here are a few of them:

❶ St. Margaret, Middle Village (1860)
❷ St. Joseph, Astoria (1878)
❸ St. Boniface, Brooklyn (1854)
❹ All Saints, Williamsburg (1868)
❺ St. Nicholas, Williamsburg (1866)
❻ B.V.M. Help of Christians, Woodside (1854)
❼ St. Fidelis, College Point (1856)
❽ Presentation of the B.V.M, Jamaica (1886)

Bishop John Loughlin (1853-1891)

❖ *Our Lady of Victory, Bedford-Stuyvesant (1868)*

❖ *This relief of St. Patrick hangs in Resurrection-Ascension, a parish founded in Rego Park in 1926.*

❖ *St. Joseph, Pacific Street, as seen in 1886.*

❖ *The parish orchestra, Holy Cross, Flatbush, ca. 1890.*

Then as now, Catholic devotional life centered on the parish. In Brooklyn, as elsewhere, a typical Sunday Mass schedule included a high Mass led by a choir usually around 10 a.m. Later in the day, Vespers (the official evening prayer of the Church) was celebrated, concluding with Benediction of the Blessed Sacrament. In 1866, the Forty Hours, a longtime staple of eucharistic devotion, came to the United States. In 1873, it was introduced to the Brooklyn Diocese at the Convent of the Visitation.

A highlight of parish life was the mission, an annual weeklong event designed to rekindle religious fervor

Bishop John Loughlin (1853-1891)

❖ *St. Mary Star of the Sea, Carroll Gardens (1855)*

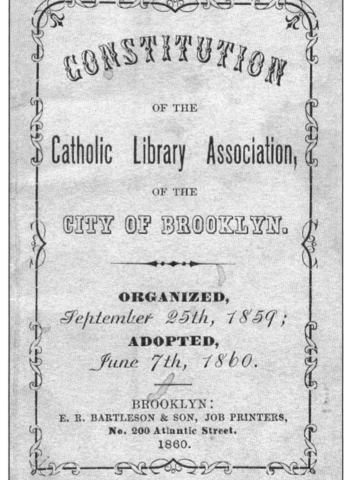

among parishioners. In his book *Catholic Revivalism*, Professor Jay Dolan notes that the mission played a key role in solidifying Catholic identity in an immigrant community. The mission featured skilled preachers from religious orders whose morning and evening talks stressed the need for the sacraments. In 1853, the Redemptorists conducted the first parish missions in the Brooklyn Diocese at St. Michael's, Flushing. In 1856, they ran a mission at St. Mary Star of the Sea in Far Rockaway.

The Growth of Parish Societies

Throughout the year, parish societies helped foster Catholic life. A dizzying variety of confraternities and societies emerged during the 1800's, each with a specific emphasis. Some were dedicated to the Immaculate Heart of Mary, others to the Rosary, still others to the Infant Jesus and to St. Joseph. In 1872, Brooklyn's first Holy Name Society was established at St. Paul's parish on Court Street. Groups such as the Holy Name Society helped create stronger bonds among laypeople through their communal vision of life.

While some groups were strictly devotional, others strove to meet the intellectual, social and recreational needs of their members.

From Brooklyn to Suffolk, parishes formed debating unions, drama societies and mutual aid societies. Some formed temperance societies whose members abstained from alcohol. While Father William Keegan was Pastor of Assumption parish in Brooklyn Heights (1855-1890), the Guild of the Confraternity of the Holy Cross maintained a parish library for children, and provided material assistance for its sick members. At St. Peter's parish on Hicks Street, the Library Association sponsored a lecture series that featured renowned ecclesiastic and civic

YOUNG MEN'S Catholic Library Association,
(Attached to St. Patrick's Church,)
EAST BROOKLYN.
Large selection of interesting and useful books.
Library open every Sunday from 2 P. M. to 4 P. M.
Members meet the first Tuesday of each month.

❖ *The Young Men's Catholic Library Association, 1869.*

Bishop John Loughlin (1853-1891)

❖ *St. Mark, Sheepshead Bay (1861)*

❖ *Sacred Heart, Bayside (1878)*

❖ *Sacred Heart, Fort Greene (1871)*

❖ *Our Lady of the Presentation, Brownsville (1887)*

leaders. Its 1872 series featured Bishop Patrick Lynch of Charleston and Louis Lowe, the former governor of Maryland. Because the parish was unable to accommodate the crowds, the lectures were moved to the nearby Brooklyn Academy of Music.

Beyond their social aspect, fraternal societies in nineteenth century America offered members an important practical benefit, life insurance for their families. When Catholic immigrants arrived, many of the societies they encountered were non-Catholic, if not anti-Catholic. As a result, several Catholic fraternal organizations were organized during the late nineteenth century, many of them short-lived. One of these was the Catholic Benevolent Legion, formed in Brooklyn in 1881. The most successful and long lasting, however, was the Knights of Columbus, founded in Connecticut in 1882 by Father Michael J. McGivney. In 1891, the first council in New York State, Brooklyn Council No.60, was formed at Hartung's Hall, on Fifth Avenue and 19th Street.

The Spirituality of the Immigrant Church

The nineteenth century has been called the "century of the Sacred Heart." After Pope Pius IX universalized the feast in 1856, devotion to the Sacred Heart of Jesus grew throughout the Catholic world. Perhaps the emphasis on Christ's suffering explains its appeal to immigrants whose own lives involved many hardships. Many of the metropolitan area parishes

named for the Sacred Heart were established during this time. Two local examples are Sacred Heart in Fort Greene, founded in 1871, and Sacred Heart in Bayside, founded in 1878. On December 8, 1873, at St. James Cathedral, Bishop Loughlin consecrated the Diocese of Brooklyn to the Sacred Heart.

Throughout the Catholic world in the nineteenth century, there was a revival of Marian devotion. Marian apparitions in France, to St. Catherine Laboure in 1830 (which inspired the Miraculous Medal devotion), at LaSalette in 1846, and at Lourdes in 1858, strengthened Mary's place in Catholic life. Countless societies and religious communities dedicated themselves to the Blessed Mother. In 1846, the American bishops petitioned Rome that Mary be named the Patroness of the Republic, under the title of the Immaculate Conception. Catholic ethnic groups honored Our Lady under various titles. While devotion to Our Lady of Mount Carmel was strong among Italian Catholics, Our Lady of Czenstochowa occupied a central place in Polish Catholic life. For immigrant Catholics, Mary was a symbol both of purity and hope.

Catholic devotionalism was not exempt from criticism, either from within or outside the Church. It was critiqued both in the secular press and by Catholic leaders who warned against identifying the faith with

❖ *Above: Father Isaac Hecker, C.S.P. (1819-1888) preached numerous parish missions throughout the Brooklyn Diocese.*

exterior practices of piety. Leading converts such as Father Isaac Hecker, founder of the Paulists, and Orestes Brownson, the century's preeminent American Catholic intellectual, urged Catholics to internalize their faith more deeply. For Hecker and Brownson, this was the first step toward a more effective apologetic. Only in this way, they argued, could the Church be capable of effectively evangelizing the nation.

The Rise of the Catholic Press

For the historian of nineteenth century Brooklyn Catholicism, newspapers are frequently the only available source. Brooklyn Catholic life was a popular topic in the New York newspapers. From Manhattan to Sag Harbor, dailies and weeklies closely followed the Church's progress. From 1841 to 1955, the *Brooklyn Daily Eagle* was a nationally renowned paper whose prestige ensured that Brooklyn Catholic news received national attention.

Catholic journalism in New York began in 1825 with the *Truth Teller*, a lay-operated weekly. Among its contributors were Father Joseph Schneller, the third pastor of St. Paul's in Brooklyn, and FATHER FELIX VARELA, the Cuban-born Vicar General of the New York Diocese. Both of them disassociated themselves from the paper when it actively promoted lay trusteeism. After the paper folded in 1855, other attempts at a local Catholic paper included the *Metropolitan Record* (1857-1862) and the *New York Tablet* (1859-1864). These were privately funded operations, and the lack of institutional support ensured their short existence.

The history of the nineteenth century New York Catholic press was intimately connected with the careers of three Brooklynites. JAMES A. MCMASTER (1820–1886), a convert, was the often controversial editor of the *Freeman's Journal*, the century's most popular Catholic newspaper. A parishoner of St. Patrick's parish on Kent Avenue, his daughter Helen Pauline joined the Discalced Carmelites. In 1907, as Mother Teresa of Jesus, she founded the first Carmelite monastery in Brooklyn. During the Civil War, the War Department suspended McMaster's paper because of his outspoken advocacy of states' rights and his criticism of President Lincoln's wartime leadership.

MAURICE FRANCIS EGAN (1852-1924) lived in Brooklyn during the 1880's, when he succeeded McMaster as editor of the *Freeman's Journal*. A man of many talents, Egan served as the United States Ambassador to Denmark and taught English at the University of Notre Dame. For a time, Egan was also associated with the *Catholic Review*, a Brooklyn-based paper that chronicled the Catholic life in the metropolitan area.

PATRICK VALENTINE HICKEY (1846-1889) came to Brooklyn from Ireland at the age of twenty. In 1872, he founded the *Catholic Review* to chronicle the progress of the Church worldwide and to offer an American Catholic apologetic. His other publications included the weekly *Illustrated Catholic American* (1880) and the *Catholic American* (1888). A father of nine children, Hickey was a deeply pious man who attended daily Mass, made frequent visits to the Blessed Sacrament, and was a strong proponent of the family rosary. His early death shocked Catholic New York, and his funeral Mass was celebrated at St. Paul's parish on Court Street.

❖ The Brooklyn Catholic, *1869*.

❖ The Catholic Review, *1872.*

❖ *Dedication Ceremony for the Cathedral of the Immaculate Conception, 1868.*

In 1869, Fathers Edward Fitzpatrick and Thomas Gardiner founded Brooklyn's first diocesan newspaper, the *Brooklyn Catholic*. During its brief existence, it gave close attention to the First Vatican Council, which was then meeting in Rome. One of the main issues addressed at the council was the question of papal infallibility. This issue became a major reason for the paper's early demise as the two priest-editors took opposing views on it. In 1870, one of them withdrew from the paper and the other died soon thereafter. From 1869 to 1872, Most Holy Trinity parish ran a German daily paper, *Brooklyner Presse*, which followed German news at home and abroad.

The Cathedral of "Living Stones" (1 Peter 2:5)

On Sunday afternoon, June 21, 1868, before a crowd of 25,000, Bishop Loughlin dedicated the cornerstone for the Cathedral of the Immaculate Conception. Numerous civil and religious dignitaries attended the ceremony, including Archbishop John McCloskey of New York. A native of Brooklyn, in 1875 McCloskey would become the first American Cardinal. The cathedral's architect was Patrick C. Keely, an Irish immigrant who came to Brooklyn in 1842. Over half a century, Keely designed over 700 churches throughout North America.

The Cathedral, however, would never be completed. The only sections finished were St. John's, the Cathedral Chapel, which remained in place until 1931, and the episcopal residence, now the Brothers' residence at Bishop Loughlin High School. Bishop

❖ *Artistic rendering of the proposed Cathedral, 1959.*

Loughlin's attention was directed toward the more pressing needs of the day: orphaned children, the aged and the sick, the poor and the needy. New parishes

Bishop John Loughlin (1853-1891)

❖ *Mother De Chantal at St. John's Home, ca. 1890.*

❖ *St. Vincent's Home, 1944.*

needed to be built for a growing Catholic population, and schools for their children.

In 1853 Bishop Loughlin found only two organizations caring for needy children and the poor. The first was the Roman Catholic Orphan Asylum Society, which oversaw three orphanages. The second organization was the Emerald Benevolent Association of the City of Brooklyn, organized by a group of twenty laymen in 1839. That year they organized a dinner dance to raise money for Catholic childcare on Long Island. In 1853, the group's name was changed to the Emerald Association. The annual Emerald Ball, currently in its 164th year, is the longest running charity function of its kind in the United States.

The St. Vincent de Paul Society, founded in Paris in 1833, erected its American branch in 1845 in

St. Louis. Ten years later, Bishop Loughlin organized the society's St. James Conference in Brooklyn. Its activities included teaching catechism, legal advocacy for the poor, visiting the sick, burying the dead, and collecting funds for charity. In 1869, St. Vincent's Home for Boys opened under its jurisdiction. The home's goal was to provide homeless boys with the needed background and skills to enter society. The Society's members were among the first to recommend building a Catholic hospital in Brooklyn.

In 1869, the *Brooklyn Daily Eagle* applauded Bishop Loughlin's decision to open St. Vincent's Home, a residence home for poor working boys, many of whom worked for the *Eagle*. Located

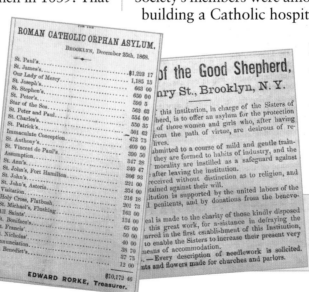

❖ *Contributions to the R.C. Orphan Asylum Society, 1869*

❖ *In 1868, the Sisters of the Good Shepherd founded a home for young women in Brooklyn.*

PATRICK C. KEELY (1816 - 1896)

As a draftsman, carver and architect, Keely designed some 700 church buildings. His work can be seen throughout the United States and in Canada. He and his wife Sarah had 17 children. Several of them died in infancy, while others entered their father's profession. In a recent address on Keely's legacy, Edward H. Furey, the President of the Keely Society, has noted the many outstanding tributes paid to the architect at the time of his death. One in particular stands out, a reflection by his friend Father Malone, who preached at Keely's funeral Mass:

Patrick Charles Keely, was indeed a man who, for fifty years, honored and served God as fervently as priest or bishop at the altar. His thoughts were constantly on God and on His sanctuary. He had genius, inspiration and the stimulus of Catholic principles and of the Catholic Faith deep down in his soul. His was a great missionary work, and we would be unworthy of the Celtic race, unworthy of benediction, were we to allow the memory of such a man to perish.

Patrick Charles Keely was born in Tipperary, Ireland, in 1816. At age 26, he came to New York, settling in Williamsburg. His earliest architectural work was a carved altar and reredos for St. James Church. He also worked on the renovation of St. Mary's Church, which was renamed SS. Peter and Paul in 1848. The pastor, Father Sylvester Malone, became a lifelong friend of Keely.

Patrick Charles Keely is buried in Holy Cross Cemetery, Brooklyn. Ironically, only a small stone slab marked "Keely" indicates his grave, a decided contrast to the many grandiose structures he built across North America.

❖ *The St. Vincent De Paul Society sponsors a Christmas dinner for the poor, 1887.*

❖ *Orphaned children at the Convent of Mercy, ca. 1885.*

BROOKLYN'S RELIGIOUS

Under Bishop Loughlin, the Diocese experienced tremendous growth. Much of this success was due to the religious communities that established Brooklyn foundations during this period. Seen here are a few of the men and women's religious communities that first made their mark on our Diocese under Loughlin.

THE SISTERS OF ST. DOMINIC

In August 1853, four Dominican nuns from Bavaria arrived in the port of New York, on their way to St. Vincent's Abbey in Pennsylvania. When their plans were sidetracked, Father Johann Raffeiner brought them to Most Holy Trinity parish in Williamsburg, where they established their motherhouse and took over the parish school. In 1857, they accepted their first novice from the parish. During their first forty years in the Diocese, there were over 300 Sisters running 19 schools, 12 orphanages and one hospital.

THE SISTERS OF ST. JOSEPH

Founded in France in 1650, the Sisters of St. Joseph opened their first American foundation, in Missouri, in 1836. In August 1856, Sister Mary Austin Kean began Brooklyn's first Josephite foundation, St. Mary's Convent and Academy, in Williamsburg. In 1860, the Josephites established their motherhouse in Flushing, along with a novitiate and boarding school. By 1891, 210 Josephites operated over thirty schools, several orphanages, and St. John's Hospital in Long Island City.

THE SISTERS OF MERCY

Founded in Ireland in 1831, the Sisters of Mercy came to Manhattan in 1846. In 1855, Mother Mary Vincent Haire brought five sisters across the river to Brooklyn, where they opened the Convent of St. Francis of Assisium on Jay Street. In 1862, the Sisters opened their motherhouse in Fort Greene, across the street from St. Patrick's parish. When they came to Brooklyn, the Sisters taught at St. James parochial school, visited the sick and provided religious instruction for those imprisoned in city jails. They soon expanded their mission to include an orphanage and an industrial school for girls. In the 1890's they opened St. Mary of the Angels Home in Syosset and Angel Guardian Home in Brooklyn.

SISTERS ADORERS OF THE PRECIOUS BLOOD

This contemplative community of prayer arrived in the Diocese on December 4, 1889. In addition to its mission of prayer and penance, it also included retreats for young women. The Confraternity of the Precious Blood was established in 1891.

Bishop John Loughlin (1853-1891)

THE SISTERS OF THE VISITATION OF MARY

Founded in 1610 by St. Jane Frances de Chantal and St. Francis de Sales, the Sisters established their first American foundation in 1799. After coming to Brooklyn in 1855, they opened the Academy of the Visitation, a preparatory school for young girls. The Sodality of the Children of Mary was begun at the monastery in 1865, and in 1883 the Archconfraternity of the Guard of the Sacred Heart was established there. At the turn of the century, the Sisters bought property in Bay Ridge, where this cloistered community continues to work "solely for the glory of God."

THE VINCENTIAN FATHERS AND BROTHERS

Founded in 1625 by St. Vincent De Paul, the Congregation of the Mission opened its first New York foundation in 1842, at St. Joseph's Seminary in the Fordham section of the Bronx. In 1868, the Vincentians opened St. John the Baptist parish, Bedford-Stuyvesant, which they named in honor of Bishop Loughlin. St. John's College (now St. John's University) opened next to the church in 1870, followed by St. John's Preparatory School. In 1891, St. John's Seminary opened on the parish grounds. By the time of Bishop Loughlin's death, St. John's had become a powerhouse of Brooklyn Catholic life. Relocated to Queens in 1954, St. John's University is the largest Catholic university in the United States.

THE FRANCISCAN BROTHERS OF BROOKLYN

In 1858, Brothers John McMahon and Vincent Hayes came from Ireland to found the Brooklyn Congregation of the Regular Third Order of St. Francis. Over the next four decades, the new community opened two high schools, fifteen parochial schools, and St. Francis College, Long Island's first Catholic college. By 1891, there were 82 Brothers involved in the educational apostolate and childcare. Today they staff the largest Catholic high school in the United States, St. Francis Preparatory School in Fresh Meadows.

THE CHRISTIAN BROTHERS

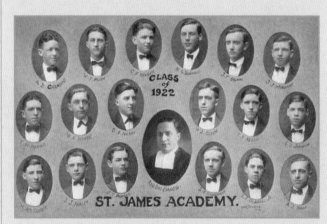

In 1851, the Christian Brothers came from Manhattan to teach at St. James parochial school. In 1883, the school program was expanded to include a high school, which they named St. James Academy. St. James was Long Island's first Catholic high school. Its students were known as the "Boys of Jay Street." In 1933, it was moved to Fort Greene and was renamed Bishop Loughlin Memorial High School.

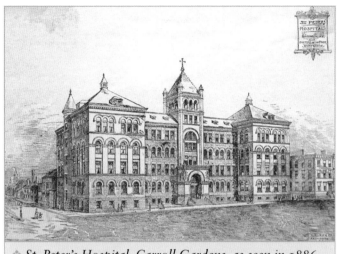

❖ *St. Peter's Hospital, Carroll Gardens, as seen in 1886.*

❖ *St. Catherine's Hospital, Williamsburg, was founded in 1870.*

❖ *Little Sisters of the Poor Bread Wagon, ca. 1910.*

St. Joseph's Institute for the Improved Instruction of Deaf Mutes.

It is quite characteristic of our worthy Bishop of Brooklyn to accomplish his great works quietly and unostentatiously. His fatherly care extends to all his people, the young and the old, the afflicted as well as those in the possession of all their faculties. Under his wise and fostering care the charitable institutions of the diocese have become a pattern for other dioceses. A few years ago there was no place nearer than Fort Washington, N. Y., where a deaf mute could receive instruction ; and that too, a Protestant institution, where hatred of all things Catholic seemed to be the first lesson impressed upon the too susceptible minds of the poor children of Catholic parents. This evil has been partially remedied by the establishment of St. Joseph's Institute, 510 Henry street, where deaf mute girls are taught the practice of their holy religion as well as the different branches of a secular education, how to do house work, plain and fancy needle work, etc. But few are aware of how thoroughly the work of instruction is carried on ; the principal, Miss Phalen, is a religious who has devoted her whole time and attention to this work. The Institute is managed by a society of ladies who are bound by the same vows as any of the other orders of Sisters. One peculiarity of this order is that its members are obliged to be known by the same names

St. Mary's Female Hospital,
OF THE
CITY OF BROOKLYN,

Has been recently incorporated, under the General Laws of the State of New York, with the object of affording Medical and Surgical aid to those suffering from Diseases Peculiar to Women.

The great necessity and usefulness of an institution such as this has long been felt by those most capable of judging, namely, members of the medical profession.

It is proposed, so far as means will permit, to provide board and medicine for all patients who are unable to pay, and to charge a moderate sum to those only who can afford it. There will be also an out-door department, where, during certain hours of the day, advice, medicine, and surgical treatment may be had on application, and free of charge.

The nursing and interior management will be under the charge of the Sisters of Charity, who have kindly volunteered their very valuable and efficient services.

A house and lot have been purchased, with procurable rear space enough for the erection of such additional buildings as may be required.

As all patients will be treated without preference or distinction of either country or religion, the Managers appeal with confidence to the public generally for aid in establishing and maintaining this great charity.
Respectfully,

CORNELIUS DEVER, 139 Clinton St., or 109 Pearl St.,
EDWARD HARVEY, 122 Livingston Street.
DANIEL McCABE, 57 South Oxford St.
P. F. O'BRIEN, Bedford Av., bet. Park and Myrtle Av.
WILLIAM TOBIN, 228 Union St. *Managers.*

P. S.—Donations and Subscriptions forwarded to either of the Managers ; the Sisters of Charity in charge at the hospital, 155 Clinton Street, or to Dr. BYRNE, 202 Clinton Street, will be promptly and gratefully acknowledged.
Brooklyn April 1868

❖ *Left : St. Joseph's School for the Deaf.*
❖ *Right : St. Mary's Hospital.*

on Poplar Street near the *Brooklyn Eagle*'s office, St. Vincent's Home was better known as the "Newsboys' Home." Loughlin placed the St. Vincent de Paul Society in charge of the home. It provided for the social, pastoral and educational needs of its charges. In 1906, the home moved to its current location in Boerum Hill. For 135 years St. Vincent's Services, as it is now known, has served the needs of children in the metropolitan area.

Childcare was a prime focus of Catholic charity under Bishop Loughlin and his successors. In 1853, only one religious community, the Sisters of Charity, was involved in childcare. New religious communities entering the Diocese responded to this pressing need. In 1868, the Sisters of St. Joseph established St. John's Home on Albany Avenue. The Sisters of St. Dominic came to Brooklyn from Germany in 1853. By the 1890's they were operating a dozen orphanages in German parishes. By the end of Loughlin's episcopate, there were 24 Catholic

orphanages throughout Long Island serving nearly five thousand children.

The care of the elderly and handicapped was another important priority. In September 1868, the Congregation of the Little Sisters of the Poor opened its first American foundation on DeKalb Avenue, the Home for the Aged Poor. In May 1874, the Daughters of the Heart of Mary opened Brooklyn's first school for the deaf, St. Joseph's. Bishop Loughlin assigned Father Thomas Ward to study sign language, and in 1886 Ward organized the St. Joseph's Union of Deaf Mutes.

In 1864, St. Peter's Hospital, Long Island's first Catholic hospital, opened in connection with the parish on Hicks Street. It grew out of a home that

Bishop John Loughlin (1853-1891)

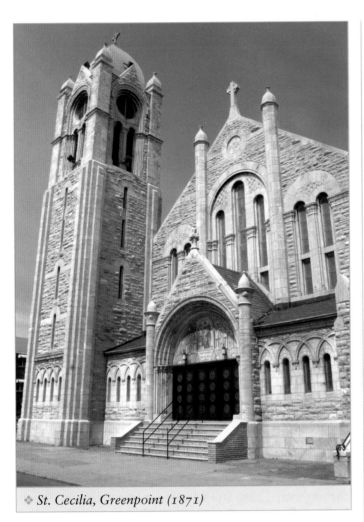

❖ *St. Cecilia, Greenpoint (1871)*

❖ *St. John's Cemetery, Middle Village (1881)*

tour of these cemeteries offers a unique insight into the early history of the Diocese.

Instead of finishing the new cathedral, Bishop Loughlin focused his attention on the pressing needs of the day. Again, Bishop Loughlin did not focus his attention on constructing a new cathedral in stone. Rather, he focused on building a cathedral of "living stones." These stones were the schools, hospitals, orphanages, homes for the aged that he erected, a system which thrives to this day. In his history of the Diocese, Monsignor Sharp writes: "John Loughlin must be set down as a pioneer bishop in modern American social relief."

The Immigrants

During the Loughlin years, Long Island's Catholic population grew from about 50,000 to nearly 300,000. The rise of Catholicism on Long Island was frequently noted in the press. In December 1877, the *Boston Christian Register* commented: "Brooklyn… might well be called a Catholic city. The Roman Church here has more houses of worship than any other." In 1880, the *London Tablet* made a similar observation. Catholic growth on Long Island, of course, was due mainly to immigration. During Loughlin's episcopate, most of the Diocese's immigrants came from Germany and Ireland. Toward the end of his tenure, new immigrant groups were entering the Diocese, from countries such as Italy, Poland and Lithuania. Smaller communities of Czech, French and Scandinavian immigrants also began to emerge in Brooklyn.

During the late nineteenth century, an event occurred which historians Frederick Binder and David Reimers

the pastor, Father Joseph Fransioli, had established for the orphans of Civil War soldiers. Fransioli invited the Franciscan Sisters of the Poor to run the hospital. In 1868, the Sisters of Charity opened St. Mary's Hospital in Brooklyn. Two years later, the Dominican Sisters opened St. Catherine's Hospital in Williamsburg. St. John's Hospital, the first Catholic hospital in Queens, opened in 1891, shortly before Bishop Loughlin's death.

The expansion of the cemeteries system was another pressing concern. In 1822, Peter Turner's circular called for a Catholic cemetery. After St. James Cemetery was filled to capacity in 1849, Bishop John Hughes purchased land in Flatbush for a new one. Holy Cross Cemetery's first burial occurred in July 1849. In June 1855, Bishop Loughlin blessed its Chapel of the Resurrection. Holy Cross holds the remains of many of Brooklyn's early Catholic leaders, including Peter Turner. In 1881, Bishop Loughlin consecrated St. John's Cemetery in Middle Village. A

Bishop John Loughlin (1853-1891)

❖ *St. Casimir, Fort Greene (1875)*

❖ *Our Lady of Sorrows, Corona (1872)*

❖ *St. Elizabeth, Ozone Park (1873)*

❖ *Sacred Hearts of Jesus and Mary, Carroll Gardens, ca. 1905.*

call the "city's transportation revolution." Faster electric street cars, followed by the subway system, made New York City a smaller place. In 1883, the Brooklyn Bridge was completed, followed by the Manhattan Bridge in 1903 and the Williamsburg Bridge in 1909. Immigrants could move out of overcrowded Manhattan into neighboring boroughs. New immigrant neighborhoods emerged in the Bronx, in Brooklyn and throughout Long Island.

During the nineteenth century, two types of parishes were founded throughout the United States. "Territorial" parishes served the English-speaking Catholics (most of whom were Irish at that time) in a specific geographic area. The boundaries of "national parishes," on the other hand, were more fluid, serving a particular ethnic group over a wider area. By the end of Bishop Loughlin's tenure, parishes throughout Long Island were ministering to Polish, Italian, German, French and Lithuanian Catholics. Brooklyn's first Polish parish, St. Casimir, was established in 1875. Nine years later, Sacred Hearts of Jesus and Mary was created as the first parish to serve Brooklyn's growing Italian community.

The Rise of Catholic Education

When Bishop Loughlin came to Brooklyn, there were fifteen parochial schools. By 1891, there were 125 parochial schools and academies, with a student population of nearly 35,000. Nearly 1,000 religious administered and taught in these schools. (The religious communities are treated at length in a separate section of this chapter.) At the Third Plenary Council of Baltimore in 1884, the American Bishops mandated that pastors establish parochial schools whenever possible. Throughout the history of American Catholicism, education has played a central role in the Church mission to engage and transform American culture. Catholic schools have also played a key role in helping immigrants and their children assimilate to America.

IMMIGRANT PRIESTS IN AN IMMIGRANT DIOCESE

FATHER JULES JOLLON

Born in France, Father Jules Jollon founded St. Louis, Brooklyn's only French parish, in 1869. He served as pastor until his death in 1912. He is seen here wearing medals awarded him by the French government for his ministry to French Catholics abroad

MONSIGNOR THOMAS TAAFFE

A graduate of All Hallows in Ireland, Monsignor Thomas Taaffe came to Brooklyn in 1863. He was pastor of St. Patrick, Kent Avenue, for 48 years. In 1882, his brother James came from Ireland to serve as his curate.

FATHER JOSEPH BRUNEMANN, O.S.F.

Born in Holland, Father Joseph Brunnemann was a Dutch Franciscan who came to Brooklyn in 1854. In 1868, he became the first resident pastor of St. Mary Star of the Sea, Far Rockaway.

FATHER NICHOLAS BALLEIS, O.S.B.

Ordained in Salzburg in 1831, Nicholas Balleis was an Austrian Benedictine who served Bedford-Stuyvesant's German Catholics at St. Francis-in-the-Fields parish from 1866 to 1888.

FATHER JOSEPH FRANSIOLI

Born in Switzerland, Father Joseph Fransioli came to Brooklyn in 1856. In 1859, he founded St. Peter's Church on Hicks Street.

MONSIGNOR MICHAEL MAY

Born in Germany, Michael May was Bishop Loughlin's Vicar General and Pastor of Most Holy Trinity, Williamsburg. In 1893 he became the first Brooklyn priest to be named a Monsignor.

MONSIGNOR JOSEPH MCNAMEE

Ordained in 1869, Monsignor Joseph McNamee founded St. Teresa of Avila, Prospect Heights, in 1874. He served as pastor for 53 years.

This stained glass window is from Our Lady of Lourdes, Queens Village (1924).

CHAPTER THREE

"Building the Kingdom of God on Long Island": Bishop Charles E. McDonnell (1892-1921)

A New Bishop

After Bishop Loughlin's death, Archbishop Michael Corrigan of New York appointed Father Michael May, the Vicar General, as Diocesan Administrator. On February 27, 1892, it was announced that Monsignor Charles Edward McDonnell, Chancellor of the New York Archdiocese, had been appointed the second Bishop of Brooklyn. On April 25, McDonnell was consecrated at the new St. Patrick's Cathedral on Fifth Avenue. On May 2, he formally took possession of the Diocese of Brooklyn at St. James Cathedral. At age 37, he was the youngest bishop in the United States.

Before coming to Brooklyn, Bishop McDonnell had an impressive background. Born in Manhattan in 1854, he graduated from the College of St. Francis Xavier on West Sixteenth Street and studied at the North American College. He was ordained in Rome in 1878. After six years of parish ministry, he was appointed secretary to Cardinal John McCloskey. After McCloskey's death in 1885, he stayed on as Archbishop Corrigan's secretary. In 1889, he became Chancellor of the Archdiocese, and in 1890 he was named one of the first Monsignors in the United States.

❖ *Former President Theodore Roosevelt (third from left) visits St. Patrick's Rectory, Huntington, 1912.*

Contemporaries described McDonnell as cultured, elegant and witty. At the same time he was also methodical, conservative and extremely private. His dislike for the

Bishop Charles E. McDonnell (1892-1921)

❖ *Father McDonnell's ordination card, Rome, 1878.*

❖ *Bishop McDonnell at the time of his consecration, 1892.*

❖ *This tabernacle is from St. Gabriel, East New York (1901).*

public eye seemed to border on a phobia at times, and he shunned publicity at all costs. In 1917, when America entered World War I, he agreed to participate in a fund drive, but only on the condition that he would not have to speak in public. Bishop McDonnell, it seems, preferred deeds to words, and his episcopate was one long testimony to that fact.

Charles McDonnell was Bishop of Brooklyn from 1892 to 1921. For both Church and nation, these were years of tremendous growth and vast changes. The Spanish-American War of 1898 marked America's arrival as a world power. By the turn of the century, the nation had emerged as the world's leading industrial producer, but prosperity brought its own perils as the gap between rich and poor widened. There were many inequities tied to economic growth, as workers labored under subhuman conditions for long hours and poor wages. As labor sought to improve its lot, strikes and riots became a frequent occurrence. Under President Theodore Roosevelt

❖ *Bishop McDonnell's episcopal coat of arms.*

(1901-1909), however, the government took the lead in fighting these and other injustices.

Father James Hennesey describes these years as "growing pains" in the American Catholic community. Between 1880 and 1900, a series of heated discussions took place among the American bishops, which focused on the need for national parishes and parochial schools, the Church's support for the labor movement, and the erection of a national pontifical university. The larger question they were debating was the meaning of Catholic identity within the American context; hence this struggle is called the "Americanist Controversy." Archbishop John Ireland of St. Paul led those bishops who stressed Catholicism's transformative influence on society, while New York's Archbishop Corrigan led those adopting a more cautious approach. In January 1899, Pope Leo XIII's Apostolic Letter *Testem Benevolentiae* cautioned the Church in America against an uncritical acceptance of the larger culture, but no individuals were singled out for condemnation.

Bishop Charles E. McDonnell (1892-1921)

❖ *St. Aloysius, Ridgewood (1892)*

❖ *St. Barbara, Bushwick (1893)*

The Americanist debates showed that by the turn of the century, American Catholicism was coming into its own. By 1900, Professor David O'Brien notes, a rising national awareness grew among American Catholics. On Thanksgiving Day, 1900, at a meeting in Manhattan, the American Federation of Catholic Societies was formed to unite all the lay organizations throughout the United States, and to provided a voice for the laity on the major issues of the day. By 1916, its national membership reached 2.5 million. In 1908, another indication of the American Church's "arrival" occurred when the Holy See

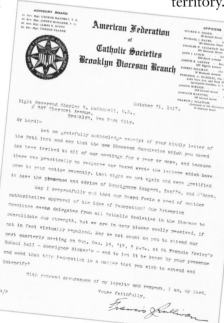

removed it from the ecclesiastical status of mission territory. Just as the United States was emerging as a world power, so too the Church in America was being recognized for its own unique ecclesial history and identity.

"The Tongues of Many Nations"

Brooklyn was developing its own unique ecclesial identity as a "Diocese of Immigrants," whose task it was to welcome the immigrant. Perhaps the biggest challenge facing young Bishop McDonnell was that of immigration. At the start of his episcopate, four out of five New Yorkers were either

Bishop Charles E. McDonnell (1892-1921)

❖ *St. Rita, Long Island City (1900)*

❖ *Our Lady of Loreto, East New York (1894)*

❖ *Immaculate Heart of Mary, Kensington (1893)*

immigrants or the children of immigrants. Between 1880 and 1920, nearly four million Catholic immigrants came to America. By 1910, there were sixteen million Catholics in the United States, as opposed to six million in 1880. During the McDonnell years, Long Island's Catholic population grew from 300,000 to 821,000.

Until 1880, most European immigrants had come from the northern and western parts of the continent; by the turn of the century, almost eighty percent were from the south and the east. No longer were the "new" European immigrants Irish and German; more often than not, they were Italian, Polish, Lithuanian, Bohemian, or Greek. But immigration was no longer confined exclusively to Europe. An Arab community was growing on Manhattan's lower East Side and would soon extend into Brooklyn. After the Spanish-

Bishop Charles E. McDonnell (1892-1921)

❖ *The Redemptorist community, Our Lady of Perpetual Help, Bay Ridge, 1903.*

❖ *St. Catherine of Alexandria, Borough Park (1902)*

American War, New York's Spanish-speaking community expanded slowly but surely. Another group coming in greater numbers were the West Indians. In his diocesan history, Monsignor John K. Sharp comments:

> *Indeed the tongues of many nations at divine worship were soon likened to the first Pentecost. Before the middle of the McDonnell administration the Gospel was being preached in 13 languages- English, German, Italian, Polish, Lithuanian, French, Scandinavian, Bohemian, Slovak, Greek, Hungarian, Arabic, and Spanish- by priests well versed in foreign tongues.*

One of the most important ways Bishop McDonnell responded to the pastoral challenges of immigration was to bring new religious orders into the Diocese. By the turn of the century, Italian Franciscans ministered to their fellow countrymen at Our Lady of Peace in Park Slope, while Polish Franciscans did the same at St. Adalbert's in Elmhurst. In 1902, Italian Vincentians established St. Rocco's in Park Slope. Spanish Vincentians established Our Lady of Pilar for Spanish-speaking Catholics in 1916. In 1897, German Capuchins took over St. Michael's, a German parish in East New York. During World War I, Slovakian Franciscans administered Holy Family parish in Greenpoint.

In 1891, there were only three orders of priests in the Diocese: the Vincentians, the Fathers of Mercy, and the Pallottines. Some of Bishop Loughlin's contemporaries alleged that he had an antipathy for religious order priests. If so, that was certainly not true of his successor, who invited ten communities to Brooklyn. At Bay Ridge in 1893, the Redemptorists founded Our Lady of Perpetual Help. Three years later, the Benedictines established St. Killian in Farmingdale. In 1904, the Montfort Fathers established Mary Gate of Heaven in Ozone Park. In 1908, the Jesuits founded St. Ignatius

❖ *Born in France, Montfort, Father René LeClair founded Mary Gate of Heaven, Ozone Park, in 1904.*

BROOKLYN'S POLISH PARISHES

Seen here are a few of the 15 Polish parishes that Bishop McDonnell founded.

❶ St. Josaphat, Bayside (1910)
❷ Holy Cross, Maspeth (1912)
❸ St. John Cantius, East New York (1902)
❹ St. Stanislaus Kostka, Greenpoint (1896)
❺ Our Lady of Consolation, Williamsburg (1909)
❻ SS. Cyril and Methodius, Greenpoint (1917)
❼ St. Joseph, Jamaica (1904)

❖ *Holy Cross School, Maspeth, 1917.*

Bishop Charles E. McDonnell (1892-1921)

❖ *Monsignor Boleslaus Puchalski (1870-1957)*

❖ *Fr. Casimir Zakrajsek, O.F.M., Pastor of Holy Family, Greenpoint , was honored by the Slovakian government for his work with immigrants in America.*

In addition to parishes for the Poles and Lithuanians, Bishop McDonnell established Holy Family, a Slovak parish now located on Nassau Avenue in Greenpoint, in 1903.

Hispanic Catholics

By World War I, Brooklyn's Spanish-speaking population had reached 6,000. By the turn of the century, a lay Hispanic community had formed at Assumption parish in Brooklyn Heights. Priests from St. Michael, Bay Ridge, operated a "Spanish Chapel" for Puerto Ricans living near the Navy Yard. From 1906 to 1913, Father Jose Rivera, a native of Puerto Rico, was assigned to St. Cecilia's parish. He was the first Hispanic priest to serve in the Diocese. At Visitation parish in Red

❖ *Father José Rivera (1876-1943)*

Hook, the pastor, Monsignor William J. White (who was fluent in Spanish), organized a committee of Hispanic laywomen to coordinate religious activities for the local Latino community.

In October 1916, Bishop McDonnell opened Brooklyn's first parish for Spanish-speaking Catholics, Our Lady of Pilar, on Cumberland Street. Bishop Antonio Monestel of Honduras accompanied him at the parish dedication, where a visiting Mexican priest preached the homily. McDonnell invited Spanish Vincentians from the Barcelona Province to administer the parish. Father Antonio Canas, C.M., was appointed pastor. Realizing the need for priests who could speak Spanish, McDonnell sent a few seminarians to study at the University of Salamanca in Spain.

Bishop Charles E. McDonnell (1892-1921)

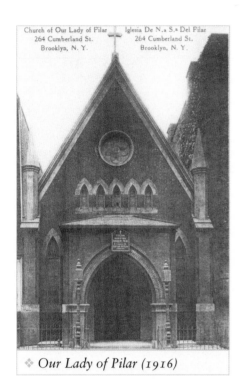

❖ *Our Lady of Pilar (1916)*

❖ *La Sociedad del Santo Nombre, Our Lady of Pilar, 1935.*

❖ *Father Bernard Quinn (top row, left) with Sunday School children at St. Peter Claver, 1920.*

African-American Catholics

By 1915, New York's African-American population was growing rapidly as Southern Blacks moved North in search of better living conditions. Although the majority were Protestant, a Black Catholic community had begun to emerge in Brooklyn. In 1915, a group of Black Catholics organized by Jules DeWeever met in the home of Sarah Walters, across the street from St. Joseph's Church in Prospect Heights. It was here that the "Colored Catholic Club of Brooklyn" was formed, and meetings were scheduled for the first and third Friday of each month.

There had been African-American Catholics in Brooklyn throughout the nineteenth century, but it was only in 1915 that they organized as a body and petitioned Bishop McDonnell for a parish of their own.

In 1920, McDonnell assigned Father Bernard Quinn to establish a parish in Brooklyn for Black Catholics. Quinn bought property on Ormond Street in Bedford-Stuyvesant (now Claver Place), where he built St. Peter Claver parish. The minutes of the Colored Catholic Club meeting on November 9, 1920, are worth quoting at length:

And whereas God in His infinite goodness and by His miraculous ways has had our Beloved and Heroic Friend and Pastor the Rev. Bernard J. Quinn who of His own choice has offered and sacrificed his amiable career, has come to us and taken this Mission among us. We do hereby acknowledge our appreciation and devotion and pledge ourselves to cooperate and support him in his energies with our helpful suggestions, constructive thought, and to the fullest extent pledge our energies subject to his command. So that we may obtain our desires and offer actions...The Establishment of a Church among us, and the defense and Propagation of the Faith among our race.

❖ *St. Peter Claver, as seen in 1942.*

Bishop Charles E. McDonnell (1892-1921)

JULES DeWEEVER (1871 – 1940)

Born in the Dutch West Indies, Jules DeWeever came to America with his family as a child. A lifelong employee of the U.S. Post Office, he was one of the key leaders in organizing Black Catholic life in Brooklyn. In 1915, he helped organize the "Colored Catholic Club of Brooklyn." Monsignor Bernard Quinn worked closely with him and the Club to promote an active lay apostolate among Black Catholics. DeWeever served as president of the St. Vincent de Paul Conference at St. Peter Claver parish for almost twenty years.

In a 1922 letter to his parishioners, Father Bernard Quinn expressed the bonds of affection that grew between him and his parishioners: "I love you, I am proud of every one of you, and I would willingly shed to the last drop my life's blood for the least among you."

❖ *Founded as an Italian parish in 1903, Our Lady of Charity, Weeksville, now serves an African-American congregation.*

Eastern Rite Catholics

Pope John Paul II has compared the Latin and Eastern Rites of the Church to the lungs of the human body. For the Church to thrive, he contends, it must breath with both lungs. In 1891, St. Elias parish was established in Greenpoint for Byzantine Rite Catholics. Bishop McDonnell established two parishes for Ukrainian Catholics: Holy Ghost, Williamsburg, in 1912, and St. Nicholas of Myra, Park Slope, in 1916.

The first Arab immigrants to New York City were overwhelmingly Syrian and Lebanese Christians who formed neighborhoods on Manhattan's lower East Side. At the turn of the century, New York's Arab community expanded outwards to Brooklyn. In 1903, Father Khairallah Stephen established Brooklyn's first

❖ *Father Paul Sanky (1877-1939)*

Bishop Charles E. McDonnell (1892-1921)

❖ *Virgin Mary, Park Slope (1910)*

❖ *St. Nicholas, Park Slope, as seen in 1966.*

❖ *St. Elias, Greenpoint, 1966.*

Maronite parish, Our Lady of Lebanon. In 1910, Syrian-born Father Paul Sanky established Brooklyn's first Melkite parish, Virgin Mary. During the parish's early years, he celebrated the Divine Liturgy in the basement of St. Paul's and St. Peter's Churches in Cobble Hill until he bought property for a church on Clinton and Amity Streets.

Catholic Charities

In his history of Brooklyn Catholic Charities, Robert Murphy writes that by 1892, 34 charitable institutions were operating in the Diocese. Bishop McDonnell saw the need for a more systematic organization to Catholic charity. On April 1, 1899, therefore, he appointed Father William J. White as Supervisor of Catholic Charities in the Diocese of

❖ *Angel Guardian Home (1899)*

Brooklyn. In 1910, Monsignor White helped organize the first meeting of the National Conference of Catholic Charities in Washington, D.C. His appointment marks the formal beginning of "Catholic Charities of the Diocese of Brooklyn," now Long Island's foremost social services institution.

Bishop Charles E. McDonnell (1892-1921)

❖ *Left: A native of France, Mother Marie Antoinette, C.I.J., brought the Congregation of the Infant Jesus to Brooklyn in 1905.*
❖ *Right: Monsignor William J. White (1870-1911)*

❖ *Left: From 1913 to 1930, Monsignor Francis J. O'Hara directed Catholic Charities.*
❖ *Right: A parishioner of St. John the Baptist, Bedford-Stuyvesant, Thomas W. Hynes was a leading figure in the St. Vincent De Paul Society for over fifty years.*

❖ *A Catholic Charities-sponsored settlement house as seen in the 1930's.*

❖ *The officers of the St. Vincent De Paul Society, St. Joseph, Pacific Street, 1914.*

ORPHAN HOME AND TRADE SCHOOL
of the Sisters of St. Dominic at Farmingdale, L. I.

❖ *From 1900 to 1942, the Sisters of St. Dominic ran Nazareth Trade School, an orphanage, in Farmingdale.*

❖ *St. Joseph's Hospital, Far Rockaway.*

Bishop Charles E. McDonnell (1892-1921)

❖ *St. Francis Preparatory School, Class of 1916.*

❖ *St. Joseph High School, 1908.*

❖ *B.V.M. Help of Christians, Woodside, 1892.*

❖ *Presentation of the B. V. M. School, Jamaica, 1910.*

in Greenpoint; they soon opened nine schools. In 1904, the Daughters of Wisdom came from France to Ozone Park, where they opened Mary Gate of Heaven School in 1904 and Our Lady of Wisdom Academy in 1910. In 1921, the Grey Nuns of the Sacred Heart opened a school at St. Joan of Arc in Jackson Heights.

New brothers' communities entered the Diocese. The Society of Mary (Marianists) was founded by St. Joseph Chaminade in 1817 as a community of brothers and

priests. In 1904, they came to Most Holy Trinity in Williamsburg, where they staffed both the parochial school and the high school. In 1909, the Brothers of the Sacred Heart, founded in France in 1821, began teaching at St. Mary Star of the Sea, Far Rockaway. The Xaverian Brothers, founded in Belgium in 1839, came to Holy Cross, Flatbush, in 1920. In their parochial schools and high schools, the brothers assumed significant roles in the education of young men.

Bishop Charles E. McDonnell (1892-1921)

❖ *Our Lady of Wisdom Academy, Ozone Park, 1916.*

❖ *Graduates of Visitation School, Red Hook, 1920.*

❖ *The first Christmas at Mount Carmel Monastery, 1907.*

❖ *Holy Cross School, Flatbush, January 1942. (Courtesy of Mrs. Carmela O'Donnell)*

❖ *Our Lady of Mount Carmel Monastery, Bedford-Stuyvesant.*

Brooklyn College

(THE COLLEGE OF ST. FRANCIS XAVIER)

1125 CARROLL STREET

Under Direction of the Fathers of the Society of Jesus.

COLLEGE COURSE

The College Course Leads to the Degree A. B. The College Is Not a Seminary, nor a Mere Preparatory School. The Courses Are the Courses of a Liberal, Classical Education, Equipping Young Men for Every Profession—Law, Medicine, Business Life or Any Other Avocation.

CLASSICAL HIGH SCHOOL

The High School Department Admits Graduates of Parochial or Public Schools, and Prepares Them by the Academic or Classical Course for Entrance to College.

NOSTRAND AVE. AND CARROLL ST.

(Nostrand Ave. and Rogers Ave. Cars Pass the College.)

REV. JOSEPH H. ROCKWELL, S.J., President

Bishop Charles E. McDonnell (1892-1921)

ACADEMY OF ST. JOSEPH

In-the-Pines

Brentwood - New York

BOARDING SCHOOL FOR YOUNG LADIES

Preparatory Collegiate   Affiliated with the State University

Complete Courses in Art, Vocal and Instrumental Music

The new fireproof main building, perfect in all its appointments, comprises: Parlors, Assembly Room, Offices, Art and Vocal Studios, Private Rooms, Study Halls, Library, Roof Gardens, etc.

Indoor and outdoor athletic games and exercises, under supervision of first-class professor.

St. Joseph's Day College for Women
286-294 WASHINGTON AVE., BROOKLYN, N. Y.

Will be prepared to admit students of the freshman and sophomore grades, on the opening of the new semester, Monday, Sept. 24. For further particulars, apply to Mother Superior, Academy of Saint Joseph, Brentwood, or to the Dean of the College, Washington avenue, Brooklyn.

❖ *St. Joseph's College, Brooklyn Campus.*

❖ *The Ordination Class of 1912, St. John's Seminary, Brooklyn.*

By the turn of the century, both St. John's College and St. Francis College were firmly established. In 1908, the Jesuits attempted to start their own college in Brooklyn. Their initial plan was for a school to be named "Crown Heights University," but they opted instead for "Brooklyn College." The college opened in September 1908, along with Brooklyn Preparatory School. From the start, Brooklyn College experienced financial troubles which forced its closure in 1921. The high school, known as "Brooklyn Prep," provided a Jesuit education for young men in Brooklyn and Queens over the next half-century.

During the early twentieth century, a larger number of women entered higher education. Catholic women's colleges in New York included Manhattanville College (1841), the College of Mount St. Vincent (1847), and D'Youville College (1908). In September 1916, the Sisters of St. Joseph opened St. Joseph's College on Clinton Avenue in Brooklyn. Father Thomas E. Molloy was appointed as the college's first president. The establishment of St. Joseph's College indicates the extent to which Brooklyn Catholics were slowly expanding into the middle class.

The Contemplative Life

In his personal life, Bishop McDonnell was a man of deep prayer who made retreats whenever possible. Bishop Loughlin welcomed two contemplative communities to Brooklyn: the Visitation Sisters in 1855, and the Sisters of the Precious Blood in 1890. In October 1907, Our Lady of Mount Carmel, the first Carmelite monastery in New York State, opened in Bedford-Stuyvesant. Bishop McDonnell had purchased the former McCann mansion for its use. McDonnell saw Brooklyn's monasteries as a powerful arm of the local Church, whose apostolate of unceasing prayer sustained the Diocese's many apostolic works.

MOTHER TERESA OF JESUS (1864-1922)

F oundress of New York's first Carmelite monastery, Helen Pauline McMaster was one of seven children born to James A. McMaster, the outspoken editor of the *Freeman's Journal*, and his wife Gertrude, in Brooklyn. Educated at the Academy of the Sisters of the Holy Child in Sharon, Pennsylvania, she was proficient in art, music, and foreign languages. On the eve of the feast of Our Lady of Mount Carmel in 1882, she entered the Carmelite novitiate in Baltimore. Two of her sisters also entered religious life. Devoted to the contemplative life, she became a leading figure in the Carmelite community. While she served as novice mistress at the Baltimore Carmel, Bishop McDonnell asked her to establish a Carmelite foundation in Brooklyn. She did so in 1907, and served there until her death in 1922.

❖ *SS. Joachim and Anne, Queens Village (1896)*

❖ *Brooklyn Catholics visit the Catholic Summer School at Cliff Haven, N.Y., ca. 1910.*

Cathedral College

W hen Bishop McDonnell came to Brooklyn, there were two hundred priests working in the Diocese. During his episcopate, the number of priests nearly tripled. Promoting vocations was one of McDonnell's main goals. He was particularly concerned that Catholic college graduates were not entering the priesthood in larger numbers. Although Bishop Loughlin had established St. John's as a major seminary in 1891, McDonnell felt there was a need for a minor seminary that would nurture priestly vocations. There had been a previous attempt in 1856, when Father Bonaventure Keller, a German-born Franciscan, established a minor seminary at St.

Bishop Charles E. McDonnell (1892-1921)

❖ *Epiphany, Williamsburg (1905)*

❖ *Mass at St. John the Baptist, Bedford-Stuyvesant, in the 1940's.*

❖ *Parish procession, St. Michael, East New York, 1905.*

the Sacred Heart, various confraternities and Third Orders provided a spiritual strength and social cohesiveness to every parish community.

From its modest beginnings at St. Paul's parish in 1872, the Holy Name Society had grown considerably. In 1882, a Diocesan Union of Holy Name Societies was formed, the first in the United States. In addition to its spiritual and fraternal goals, the Holy Name Society also gave Catholic men the chance to publicly demonstrate their faith at large public rallies. In 1897, nine thousand members held a rally in Brooklyn, the first of its kind in the United States. In 1901, thousands gathered for an open-air rally in Huntington. By 1917, the Diocesan Union had 45,000 members in 175 parishes across Long Island.

❖ *First communion certificate, St. Matthew, Crown Heights (1918).*

Soon after coming to Brooklyn, Bishop McDonnell gave his formal approval to the Knights of Columbus. William Harper Bennett organized Brooklyn's Columbus Council in 1895. Two years later he organized the Long Island Chapter, to coordinate activities throughout the Diocese. Bennett was a nationally recognized leader in the order. He was instrumental in creating its Fourth Degree. By 1917, there were 55 councils in the Diocese, with a membership of 15,000. In May 1903, Brooklyn's Morning Star

Bishop Charles E. McDonnell (1892-1921)

Brooklyn Diocesan Union
—of the—
...Holy Name Society...

Brooklyn, N. Y., December 26th, 1917

Reverend dear Father:

As a timely act of adoration, thanksgiving and reparation to the Holy Name of Our Lord Jesus Christ, which is indeed above all names, and amongst men the most abused of all, and in Solemn Commemoration of the mystery in which the Holy Name was first given; the Right Reverend Bishop has arranged that a Solemn High Mass be celebrated at St. James' Pro-Cathedral at 11 o'clock, on the feast of the Circumcision, and that each Holy Name Society be represented by a delegation of its members.

The Right Reverend Bishop will preside at the Mass and the Reverend Terence J. Shealy, S. J., will preach.

You are kindly requested to send a representation from your Society as it is a Holy Name celebration.

Very sincerely yours in the Holy Name,

PETER DONOHUE,

JOSEPH R. GARVEY, Secretary   Spiritual Director

DEDICATION OF THE

Church of St. John the Baptist,

BROOKLYN, N. Y.

Trinity Sunday, May 20, 1894.

10:30 A. M.

Blessing of Church,

BY RT. REV. CHARLES E. McDONNELL, D.D.

Solemn Pontifical Mass.

CELEBRANT: MOST REV. WILLIAM HENRY ELDER, D.D.

SERMON:

HIS EMINENCE CARDINAL GIBBONS.

7:30 P. M.

Solemn Pontifical Vespers.

CELEBRANT: RT. REV. JOHN JOSEPH HENNESSY, D.D.

SERMON:

RT. REV. JOHN AMBROSE WATTERSON, D.D.

Council introduced the first "communion breakfast" to the United States after they attended Mass at St. Paul's parish on Court Street.

Under Bishop McDonnell, Catholic laywomen took an increasingly active role in Brooklyn Catholic life. In addition to parish organizations, Catholic women organized on a wider scale. The Catholic Daughters of America, an organization of Catholic laywomen, was founded in 1903. In January 1905, the Daughters formed their first Brooklyn court. In 1914, two Brooklyn women founded the International Federation of Catholic Alumnae (IFCA), a nationwide organization of female Catholic college graduates. One of its activities was to finance the ongoing education of women religious teaching in the Diocese. In addition it made "talking books" for blind children. The

KNIGHTS OBSERVE FOURTH OF JULY

Five Thousand People Attend Their Exercises at Prospect Park.

Five thousand members of the Knights of Columbus and their friends congregated in Prospect Park on the morning of July 4 to give patriotic testimony of their adherence to and readiness to defend the principles of Liberty which emanated from that stout band of patriots, met at Philadelphia, one hundred and forty-two years before.

Preceding the exercises, the First New York Regiment of the Knights of Columbus, in command of Col. George E. Lanagan, escorted the Gloucester Camp, No. 5, U. S. W. V., commanded by Edward J. Fitzsimmons, from the Sailors and Soldiers' Monument to the bandstand, where the services were held.

The celebration began with an invocation by Sir Knight Rev. James H. Casey, of St. Augustine's Church, the lately appointed chaplain of Fort Hamilton. —————— was reverently

---

RT. REV. CHARLES E. McDONNELL, D. D.
HONORARY PRESIDENT
MRS. THOMAS E. MURRAY,
FIRST VICE-PRESIDENT
MISS JOSEPHINE M. BENNETT,
SECOND VICE-PRESIDENT
MRS. WILLIAM H. GOOD
THIRD VICE-PRESIDENT

VERY REV. MSGR. FRANCIS J. O'HARA
SPIRITUAL DIRECTOR
MISS MARY BRADY
TREASURER
MISS ANNA L. McDEVITT
RECORDING SECRETARY
MISS ELIZABETH LONERGAN
CORRESPONDING SECRETARY

Catholic Women's League
107 Greene Avenue

TELEPHONE, PROSPECT 2309

Brooklyn, N. Y.   June 28, 1919.

Rt. Rev. C. E. Mc Donnell, D.D.,

Brooklyn, N.Y.

Reverend dear Bishop:-

Enclosed is the summary of the work of the Catholic Women's League for the year ending April 30, 1919. In addition, the League raised the sum of $1,142,190. in three Liberty Loan Drives($533,0 in the 3rd.; $350,000 in the 4th and $259.000 in the recent Victory Loan Drive)m for the Red Cross, $4,725. and the United War Charities, $2,287.49.The sum of $25. was sent to the Salvation Army and evidently was greatly appreciated.

In our first Red Cross Home Nursing Class, the students all passed their examinations satisfactorilyand expressed their appreciation of the excellent lessons which were given by a representative of the Red Cross. It is unusual for this course of lessons to be given away from the Home headquarters, but the splendid facilities at Green Avenue made it possible. We have a large registration for another course in the Fall.

The League wishes me to express its deep appreciation of your interest and co-operation. It has been a great inspiration and we trust that we may be encouraged to do bigger and better things next year.

Yours faithfully,

Elizabeth Lonergan.

Corresponding Secretary.

Souvenir List of Members of Brooklyn Pilgrimage to Lourdes.

Cook's Tours

Leaving New York by Red Star Line Steamer "NOORDLAND" and American Line Steamer "PARIS."

WEDNESDAY, JULY 18, 1894.

Bishop Charles E. McDonnell (1892-1921)

HELEN McCORMICK
(1889–1937)

The daughter of a college professor, Helen McCormick attended Brooklyn's prestigious Erasmus Hall High School. She went on to graduate from St. Lawrence University and Brooklyn Law School. As a young woman she taught developmentally disabled children in the public schools while conducting night classes for immigrants in Brownsville. Admitted to the bar in 1913, she became a factory inspector for the New York State Department of Labor. In 1917, she was appointed Assistant District Attorney for Kings County. Three years later she founded the Catholic Big Sisters, a mentoring program for young women. For McCormick, this sort of personal guidance played a greater role in forming future women leaders than did institutionalized reform, or what she called "proxy charity." Auxiliary Bishop Raymond A. Kearney celebrated her funeral Mass at Queen of All Saints, Fort Greene. Nearly 20,000 mourners paid their respects, a striking testimony to her influence.

❖ *Our Lady of Solace, Coney Island (1900)*

IFCA's Brooklyn circle was active in promoting wholesome entertainment for youth.

Bishop McDonnell had a great devotion to Our Lady of Lourdes. In 1894, Father Eugene Porcile, S.P.M., the French-born pastor of St. Francis De Sales in Bushwick, organized the first Diocesan Pilgrimage to Lourdes. It was a great success, and others soon followed. In 1897, McDonnell allowed Porcile to change the parish's name to Our Lady of Lourdes. (The church is now located on De Sales Place.) Our Lady of Lourdes, along with Our Lady of Solace in Coney Island, became a local pilgrimage site for Brooklyn Catholics. Monthly devotions in these churches drew large crowds from throughout the Diocese. In an increasingly multi-ethnic diocese, devotional life offered a bond of ecclesial solidarity and unity that transcended the ethnic diversities.

Public expressions of organized Catholic life in Brooklyn included the annual Military Mass at the

Bishop Charles E. McDonnell (1892-1921)

❖ *Top: Parish theater group, Presentation of the B.V.M., Jamaica, 1915.*
❖ *Bottom: St. Andrew Avellino parish, Flushing, as seen in 1916.*

❖ *Left: Father Eugene H. Porcile, S.P.M. (1839-1912)*
❖ *Right: Monsignor William F. McGinniss (1867-1932)*

Brooklyn Navy Yard, which began in 1902. In the prewar years, this celebration drew an average of 30,000 worshippers. Parish May devotions attracted equally large crowds across Long Island. Every July, for over a century, Williamsburg has hosted a festival in honor of Our Lady of Mount Carmel and St. Paulinus, attracting thousands from throughout the metropolitan area. These events were local expressions of a growing confidence in the American Catholic community.

Anti-Catholicism, however, continued to be a significant obstacle, even after

❖ *Statue at St. Mary Magdalene, Springfield Gardens (1913).*

the demise of the Know-Nothings. During the 1890's, the American Protective Association, a nativist society dedicated to keeping Catholics out of public office, gained a local Brooklyn following. On the eve of World War I, *The Menace*, an anti-Catholic paper published in Missouri, had a nationwide circulation of 1.5 million. Some of its Brooklyn readers wrote letters to the editor complaining about the growing Catholic influence in their neighborhoods. After the war, the Ku Klux Klan returned with a stronger anti-Catholic bent. There were other threats to Catholic life besides the blatant anti-Catholicism of *The Menace* and the A.P.A. In October 1916, Margaret Higgins Sanger opened the first birth control clinic in the United States in Brownsville, where she attempted to convert Italian Catholic immigrants to her views.

❖ *In this mosaic from St. Pancras, Glendale (1904), the pastor, Msgr. Herman J. Pfeifer is seen to the right (along with his pet dog).*

A strong Catholic apologetic developed in response. Shortly after Sanger's clinic opened, Dr. James J. Walsh, a noted Catholic physician and author, began a lecture series on family life at St. Leonard's parish in Bushwick, drawing audiences of over one thousand a night. A local organization that achieved national prominence was the Metropolitan Truth Society. In 1899, at St. Francis Xavier, Park Slope, Father William McGinnis and a group of laymen formed the society to fight a growing anti-Catholicism. The society distributed apologetic literature, and answered queries from Catholics and non-Catholics. After chapters opened in Canada, it was renamed the International Catholic Truth Society. In 1909, Monsignor McGinniss launched a successful campaign to have the Board of Education revise history textbooks that portrayed the Church in a negative light. After his death in 1932, the fiery and controversial Father Edward Lodge Curran served as president until 1974.

The Brooklyn Catholic Historical Society

By the 1890's, a historical consciousness had begun to emerge among Brooklyn Catholics, as the creation of the Brooklyn Catholic Historical Society indicates. Among its leading members were Dr. Marc F. Vallette, a Brooklyn school principal, and Thomas F. Meehan, a journalist and historian who dedicated his life to preserving the early history of the Church in Brooklyn. During its brief existence, the society held lectures on various aspects of diocesan history and collected valuable artifacts which remain today in the Diocesan Archives. One of their unrealized projects was a history museum. By the turn of the century, sadly, this group had

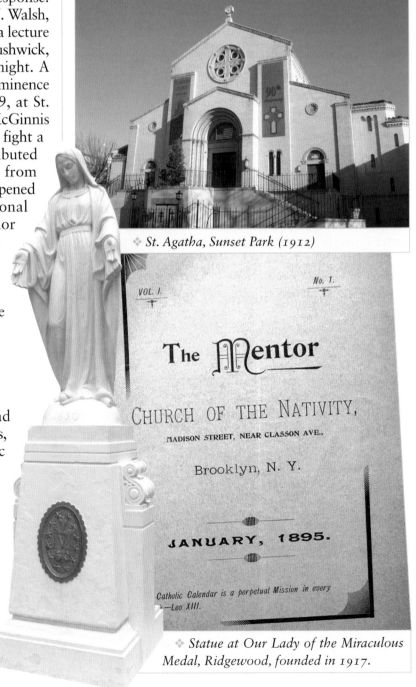

❖ *St. Agatha, Sunset Park (1912)*

VOL. I.   No. 1.

The Mentor

CHURCH OF THE NATIVITY,

MADISON STREET, NEAR CLASSON AVE.,

Brooklyn, N. Y.

JANUARY, 1895.

Catholic Calendar is a perpetual Mission in every —Leo XIII.

❖ *Statue at Our Lady of the Miraculous Medal, Ridgewood, founded in 1917.*

Bishop Charles E. McDonnell (1892-1921)

❖ *Left: Monsignor James J. Coan (1871-1926)*
❖ *Right: Thomas F. Meehan (1854-1942)*

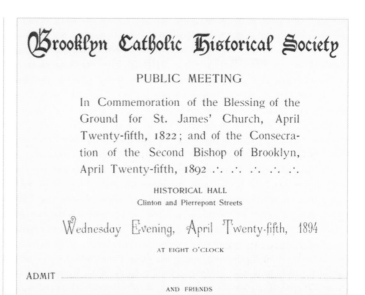

ceased to operate. Within a few years, however, *The Tablet* would pick up the task of chronicling the Brooklyn Catholic experience.

The Birth of *The Tablet*

Bishop McDonnell was encouraged by the support that he saw among the laity in favor of a Catholic newspaper. In August 1901, McDonnell received a letter from James A. Rooney of the *Brooklyn Daily Eagle* proposing a weekly diocesan newspaper, which would be "thoroughly, absolutely and aggressively Catholic." While McDonnell was a strong supporter of the Catholic press, he did not react immediately to Rooney's plans. In 1908, he appointed Father James J. Coan to edit a diocesan newspaper. McDonnell suggested *The Tablet* as its name, after the English Catholic journal that he admired. The paper's first issue was published on April 4, 1908:

> *for the greater glory of God, for the honor and expansion of our holy religion, for the conservation of loyalty and reverence for the Holy See, for the uncompromising advocacy of Catholic teaching and Catholic practice pure and undefiled, for the spiritual, intellectual and social well-being of our people.*

Within ten years, its circulation reached 25,000. No aspect of diocesan life was ignored in its pages. "From the Managing Editor's Desk" commented on the major issues of the day. "The Question Box" answered queries from readers. "The Home Circle" column gave practical suggestions for Catholic mothers and wives. There was even a column for children. Articles on

❖ The Tablet's *first issue , April 4, 1908.*

Bishop Charles E. McDonnell (1892-1921)

❖ *Left: Patrick F. Scanlan in 1917, when he started working for* The Tablet.
❖ *Right: Rev. Ward G. Meehan, U.S. Army, 1918.*

❖ *Father Thomas Sala (front row, center) as a U.S. Army Chaplain.*

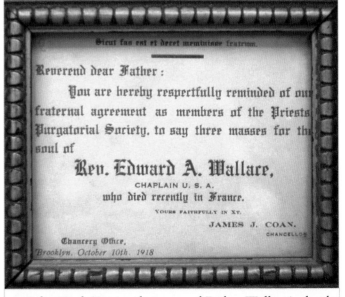

❖ *Like Mark Twain, the news of Father Wallace's death was greatly exaggerated.*

Monsignor Edward W. McCarty (1847–1925)

The first native of Brooklyn to be ordained a priest, Edward McCarty attended Brooklyn public schools and graduated from St. Francis Xavier College in Manhattan (now Xavier High School). After studying at Our Lady of the Angels Seminary, Niagara, he was ordained in June 1870. After serving at Visitation, Red Hook, and St. Peter, Carroll Gardens, he was appointed pastor of St. Augustine, Park Slope, in 1876. He remained there for nearly half a century. McCarty oversaw the construction of the present church building, long regarded as one of Brooklyn's most beautiful. An accomplished orator, he was one of the keynote speakers in October 1892 at the dedication ceremony for Brooklyn's Grand Army Plaza. Tradition has it that he celebrated the first Midnight Christmas Mass in the United States. Dedicated to Catholic education, he founded St. Augustine's High School in 1909. In May 1894, he founded the Catholic Women's Association, a Catholic counterpart to the YWCA. During the Spanish-American War McCarty was an unofficial chaplain to the troops departing for Cuba. In 1908, he was named a Monsignor. As Chairman of the Diocesan Committee on War Activities during World War I, he coordinated local Catholic activity in the interest of the war effort. By the time of his death, *The Tablet* noted, "Few major civic or patriotic events were held that did not include Msgr. McCarty as an honored guest or principal speaker."

theology, spirituality and liturgy established the paper as an important pedagogical resource. In the fall of 1917, a young teacher named Patrick F. Scanlan was appointed temporary managing editor, a post that he held for 51 years. Under his editorship, the paper would achieve national renown.

Brooklyn Catholics and World War I

In April 1917, Charles McDonnell celebrated his 25th Anniversary as Bishop of Brooklyn. That same month, the United States declared war on Germany. Nearly 40,000 Catholics from Long Island joined the Army and Navy. In Brooklyn, the Catholic Women's League operated canteens at military bases. Father Ward G. Meehan, a curate at St. Teresa of Avila in Prospect Heights, was the first Brooklyn priest to become a U.S. Army Chaplain. During the war, two dozen Brooklyn priests served in uniform. In 1918, Bishop McDonnell received word that Father Edward Wallace, a Chaplain in France, had been killed. The report turned out to be a mistake, and Father Wallace went on to serve with the Navy in World War II.

In October 1917, at The Catholic University of America in Washington, D.C., Paulist Father John J. Burke formed the National Catholic War Council (NCWC) to unite Catholic activity in the war effort. This proved to be the

Bishop Charles E. McDonnell (1892-1921)

❖ *Bishop McDonnell (center, seated) with Brooklyn seminarians, 1912. To his right is Father Thomas E. Molloy.*

❖ *St. Ephrem, Dyker Heights (1921)*

most successful organizing effort by American Catholics. After the war, it was renamed the National Catholic Welfare Council. By 1920, the American Federation of Catholic Societies ceased to exist, having been superseded by the NCWC. The NCWC was an enormous success, but it had its share of opponents, even within the ranks of the hierarchy. Bishop McDonnell, for example, felt that its activities violated canon law and posed a threat to local episcopal jurisdiction. Nonetheless, its work continued. In 1922, it was renamed the National Catholic Welfare Conference (now the U.S. Conference of Catholic Bishops).

Bishop McDonnell's Final Years

As McDonnell's health declined in later years, he petitioned the Holy See for an Auxiliary Bishop. In October 1920, Father Thomas E. Molloy became Brooklyn's second Auxiliary Bishop. On August 8, 1921, at age 67, Charles Edward McDonnell died after a long illness at the Josephite

motherhouse in Brentwood. He left a rich legacy, the most significant aspects of which are Catholic Charities, Cathedral Preparatory Seminary, *The Tablet*, and St. Joseph's College.

As an administrator, Bishop McDonnell effectively reorganized the Diocesan Curia. He initiated the Hispanic apostolate. By the end of his episcopate, the parochial school system was educating over 100,000 school children. From Williamsburg to the Hamptons, he dedicated 118 new parishes. These parishes welcomed immigrants from all over the world, Eastern Rite as well as Latin Rite Catholics, and African-Americans migrating from the South. At the time of McDonnell's silver jubilee as Bishop, *The Tablet* wrote:

He has not written his name… on the brass that corrodes or the marble that crumbles into dust. But… he has permitted it to be written large on the heart of Brooklyn Catholic life… He speaks with his heart, rather than with his lips. And it is with his heart that he has punctuated, during these last twenty-five years, the story of the growth of religious life on Long Island–and every punctuation mark is a Catholic Church.

❖ *Above: During World War I,* The Tablet *printed lists of Brooklyn Catholics then serving in the military.*
❖ *Below: This crucifix hangs in St. Virgilius, Broad Channel, one of the last parishes dedicated by Bishop McDonnell.*

Our Sacred Art

Seen here are some images of Christ found throughout our Diocese.

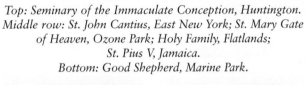

Top: Seminary of the Immaculate Conception, Huntington.
Middle row: St. John Cantius, East New York; St. Mary Gate
of Heaven, Ozone Park; Holy Family, Flatlands;
St. Pius V, Jamaica.
Bottom: Good Shepherd, Marine Park.

This painting is on the ceiling of St. Rosalia-Regina Pacis, Bensonhurst (1905).

CHAPTER FOUR

The Age of Catholic Confidence: Archbishop Thomas E. Molloy (1922-1956)

Brooklyn's Third Bishop

In August 1921, after Bishop McDonnell's death, Auxiliary Bishop Molloy was named Diocesan Administrator until Rome appointed a new ordinary. On November 21, 1921, the Holy See's Apostolic Delegate to the United States announced that Pope Benedict XV had named Thomas Molloy Brooklyn's new Bishop. Molloy was only 36 years old at the time. The news of his appointment was received enthusiastically throughout Long Island's Catholic community, where he was widely regarded and respected.

❖ *Bishop Molloy after his Consecration as an Auxiliary Bishop, July 1920.*

Thomas Edmund Molloy was born in Nashua, New Hampshire, on September 4, 1885. After graduating from St. Francis College, Brooklyn, in 1905, Bishop McDonnell sent him to the North American College in Rome, where he was ordained in September 1908. In 1909, after completing a doctorate in theology, Molloy returned to Brooklyn, where he became secretary to Auxiliary Bishop George W. Mundelein. When Mundelein was appointed Archbishop of Chicago in December 1915, Molloy accompanied him there for his first few months in office. When he returned to Brooklyn, Bishop McDonnell appointed him President of the new St. Joseph's College.

On February 15, 1922, at St. James Cathedral, Thomas Molloy was installed as Brooklyn's third Bishop. Nine days earlier, Cardinal Achille Ratti of Milan had been elected Pope Pius XI. On February 19, over 15,000 Brooklyn Catholics gathered at the 106th Regiment Armory on Bedford and Atlantic Avenues to formally welcome him. Lay representatives

Archbishop Thomas E. Molloy (1922-1956)

❖ *Bishop Thomas E. Molloy, 1934.*

❖ *In 1936, Cardinal Eugenio Pacelli visited the Brooklyn Diocese. Three years later he became Pope Pius XII (1939-1958)*

❖ *For many years,* Il Crociato *was the Diocese's Italian newspaper.*

❖ *The future Bishop Molloy (fourth from right) as a seminarian in Rome, 1908.*

from each of the Diocese's four counties delivered welcome addresses to the new Bishop, who replied that he looked forward to his new duties "hopefully, confidently and unafraid" of the challenges that the future might hold.

And the future would hold enormous challenges. For Catholics, the 1920's would witness the last outburst of organized anti-Catholicism in the Ku Klux Klan, whose national membership reached three million. The Great Depression of the 1930's nearly brought the American

Archbishop Thomas E. Molloy (1922-1956)

❖ *This painting on the ceiling of Regina Pacis, Bensonhurst, depicts Mary's Assumption.*

people to their breaking point. As the Axis powers posed an increasing threat to world peace, America entered World War II in 1941. After the war, Soviet expansion in eastern Europe initiated a Cold War lasting half a century. Postwar America experienced an unrivaled prosperity, but some important issues remained unaddressed, such as poverty and racial equality. Despite these challenges, however, this was an age of confidence for American Catholics, a belief in their ability to overcome any obstacle.

The Age of Catholic Confidence

Thomas E. Molloy was Bishop of Brooklyn from 1922 to 1956, a period that Charles Morris calls the

❖ *Bishop Molloy's episcopal coat of arms.*

HUMILITAS

SALVS ANIMARVM SVPREMA LEX

Archbishop Thomas E. Molloy (1922-1956)

❖ *A Memorial Day service at Holy Child Jesus, Richmond Hill, 1927.*

❖ *The young Bishop Molloy sits next to Mother Mary Louis, C.S.J., ca.1924.*

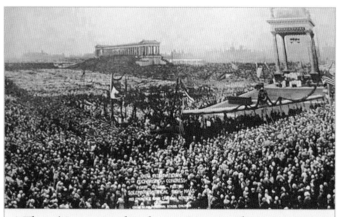

❖ *The 27ᵗʰ International Eucharistic Congress, Chicago, June 1926.*

❖ *Cardinal George W. Mundelein*

"glory days" of American Catholicism. In the years following World War I, William Halsey writes, Catholics came to see themselves as the defenders of traditional American values, which were challenged by a growing secularism. For American Catholics, the "Roaring Twenties" ushered in an era of confidence in their Church's mission to engage and to transform every dimension of the American cultural landscape. Over the next four decades, vibrant images of a triumphant Catholicism would permeate all levels of American life.

Catholics strove to apply their faith to all aspects of modern life. Academic organizations such as the American Catholic Historical Association and the American Catholic Philosophical Association brought a Catholic presence to bear on modern scholarship. Numerous organizations emerged for Catholic professionals. Between 1920 and 1960, societies were created for Catholic teachers, doctors, lawyers, nurses,

Archbishop Thomas E. Molloy (1922-1956)

❖ *Ordination Class of 1945, Seminary of the Immaculate Conception, Huntington.*

❖ The Tablet *announces the start of the seminary drive.*

❖ *Diocesan Chancery building, 75 Greene Avenue.*

and accountants. In New York City, the Holy Name Society expanded beyond the parishes to include branches for the uniformed services: the Post Office, the Fire Department, the Police Department and the Sanitation Department.

Catholic confidence was never displayed more strikingly, however, than it was in the summer of 1926. From June 20 to June 24, the Chicago Archdiocese hosted the 27th International Eucharistic Congress, the first ever held in the United States. The event drew close media attention, and the *Chicago Tribune* ran articles explaining for its readers Catholic teaching on the Eucharist. The Apostolic Delegate, Cardinal Giovanni Bonzano, traveled from New York on a special train provided by the Pullman Company. The entire train was painted red, and each door displayed Bonzano's coat of arms. On the way to Chicago, thousands greeted him and his entourage at every station.

The success of the congress was primarily due to the organizing genius of Archbishop Mundelein (who was named a Cardinal in 1924). One of its highlights was a Children's Mass at Soldier's Field, attended by 400,000 and featuring a choir of 60,000 children. On the last day of the congress, Cardinal Bonzano presided at a Pontifical Mass held on the grounds of St. Mary of the Lake Seminary, a thousand-acre campus north of the city. Over 800,000 people attended the Mass. Until World Youth Day at Denver in 1993, it was the single largest gathering of Catholics in the Western Hemisphere. Morris describes the congress as "sort of a formal debut for the American Church."

A New Seminary

Locally, a significant expression of Catholic confidence was the erection of a new seminary in Huntington. By the 1920's, the facilities at St. John's Seminary were inadequate for a growing student body. In March 1924, therefore, Bishop Molloy purchased a 200-acre estate at Lloyd's Harbor for a new

Archbishop Thomas E. Molloy (1922-1956)

❖ *Catholic Settlement House, 1940.*

he erected a new building on Greene Avenue in Brooklyn to house the Chancery and several other diocesan agencies. In 1945, he erected an office building at 191 Joralemon Street in downtown Brooklyn for Catholic Charities, the headquarters of the St. Vincent de Paul Society, the Society for the Propagation of the Faith, and the Catholic Cemeteries Office.

Catholic Charities

One of Molloy's greatest achievements was in the field of charity. By the 1920's, organized charity in the United States was going through a fundamental transformation: from a loose association of informal volunteer groups toward professional bureau-cratization. In 1920, Cardinal Patrick Hayes instituted high professional standards for Catholic charity when he organized Catholic Charities of the Archdiocese of New York. New York Charities became a model for dioceses nationwide. In her book, *Social Welfare in the Catholic Church* (1941), Dr. Marguerite Boylan wrote: "We are living in an age of organization. We must meet organization with organization."

Bishop Molloy considered this an "intelligent and practical" approach. In

❖ The Tablet *commemorates the Fiftieth Anniversary of Catholic Charities in 1949.*

❖ *Seminary of the Immaculate Conception, Huntington.*

seminary. In November 1927, he launched a fundraising campaign, which turned out to be a spectacular success. In October 1930, the Seminary of the Immaculate Conception opened (debt-free) with 85 students. On May 26, 1934, Molloy ordained 23 priests who had completed their full course of studies at Huntington. By 1953, over 500 priests had graduated from the seminary. In 1943, Bishop Loughlin's and Bishop McDonnell's remains were moved there from St. James Cathedral.

The success of the seminary campaign highlighted Bishop Molloy's effectiveness as an administrator. From the start of his episcopate, one of his primary goals was to centralize and update diocesan administration. In 1926, he founded the Central Purchasing Bureau (now Institutional Services). Four years later,

Archbishop Thomas E. Molloy (1922-1956)

DR. MARGUERITE T. BOYLAN (1887-1966)

Born in Columbus, Marguerite Boylan graduated from Ohio State University in 1913. She began her a lifelong association with Catholic Charities in Ohio, a relationship she was to continue in Connecticut and New York. From 1916 to 1931, she was Executive Secretary for Social Services in the Diocese of Hartford. In 1920, she rep-resented Hartford at the first meeting of the National Council of Catholic Women.

By the 1930's, Boylan was widely recognized as an expert on child welfare. In 1930, she was invited to the White House Conference on Child Health and Protection. The following year she was appointed Executive Secretary for Catholic Charities in the Brooklyn Diocese. She would hold that post for thirty years. In 1939, she earned a doctorate in social work from Fordham University.

Dr. Boylan taught at several schools, including Fordham University's School of Social Service and St. John's University's School of Social Action. She edited Highlights, the official publication of Brooklyn Catholic Charities. In addition to numerous articles, Boylan also wrote two books: *Social Welfare and the Catholic Church* (1941), and *They Shall Live Again* (1945). In 1947, Boylan traveled to post-war Germany as a welfare consultant for the U.S. government. Until recently, Boylan was one of the unsung heroes of Catholic Charities in the Brooklyn Diocese, but recent scholars such as Elizabeth McKeown, Dorothy Brown, and Robert Murphy have rediscovered her legacy.

1930, he appointed Monsignor J. Jerome Reddy, pastor of St. Francis De Sales, Belle Harbor, as Director of Brooklyn Charities. In 1931, the aforementioned Dr. Boylan was named Executive Secretary. After his appointment, Reddy remained pastor in Belle Harbor, while Boylan oversaw the daily operations. Over the next thirty years, they made Brooklyn Charities among the finest in the nation. Charities' priorities were childcare, health care, family life, and social action. During the 1930's, separate departments were organized to address each of these needs.

Under Reddy and Boylan, professional social workers assumed a larger role in

❖ *Monsignor J. Jerome Reddy (1888-1981)*

Charities' daily operations. They worked in orphanages, hospitals and neighborhood health centers. By 1953, one-third of all cases in the Domestic Relations Courts for Brooklyn and Queens were assigned to social workers from Catholic Charities. Through Boylan's influence, Charities sponsored scholarships for its social workers to attend Fordham University's School of Social Work. By 1940, nearly 100 of them had graduated from Fordham.

In 1925, Bishop Molloy named Monsignor Joseph F. Brophy the Diocesan Superintendent of Hospitals and Health Agencies, a position he held

Archbishop Thomas E. Molloy (1922-1956)

❖ *Our Lady of Peace Nursery, Carroll Gardens, 1944.*

❖ *St. Joseph's Hall, Bedford-Stuyvesant, 1944.*

❖ *The Mallon Employment Bureau, a Catholic Charities-sponsored program, 1944.*

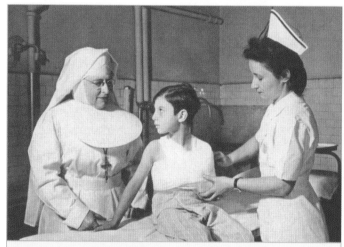

❖ *St. John's Hospital, Long Island City, 1944.*

❖ *St. John's Home, Brooklyn, 1929. In 1937 the home was moved to Rockaway Park.*

❖ *This painting depicts St. Katherine Drexel's 1930 visit to Little Flower Home, Wading River. (Courtesy of the Sisters of the Blessed Sacrament Archives, Bensalem, PA.)*

Archbishop Thomas E. Molloy (1922-1956)

❖ *Catholic Charities Court Worker, 1939.*

❖ *Mary Immaculate Hospital, Jamaica, ca. 1925.*

❖ *The Little Sisters of the Poor, Queens Village, 1944.*

❖ *Seen here as a U.S. Navy Chaplain in World II, Father Joseph Hammond directed diocesan labor schools for over thirty years.*

for 42 years. Under Brophy, hospital practices were standardized and existing facilities updated. Mary Immaculate Hospital, Jamaica, opened a new hospital building in 1929. During the 1930's, diocesan hospitals started health care centers in Brooklyn and Queens. By the 1950's, four nursing schools had been established. By the end of Bishop Molloy's episcopate, the Diocese had thirteen hospitals serving 60,000 patients. Five hundred women religious worked as nurses and administrators.

During the Great Depression, when nearly a quarter of all New Yorkers were unemployed, Catholic Charities used every means within its power to ease the plight of Long Islanders. With the help of public and private funds, Charities served as a referral agency and created work programs in the local parishes. Several religious communities, along with the Knights of Columbus, operated shelter homes and employment agencies. From 1930 to 1936, the St. Vincent De Paul Society distributed $140,000 from private sources to destitute families. Catholic Labor

Archbishop Thomas E. Molloy (1922-1956)

❖ *Our Lady of Consolation Home for the Aged, 1944.*

❖ *Bishop Molloy with officers of the Emerald Association, 1940.*

❖ *A CYO-sponsored parish dance during the 1940's.*

❖ *NBA coach Lenny Wilkins, seen here at Providence College in the 1950's, got his start in the CYO program at Holy Rosary, Bedford-Stuyvesant.*

❖ *Monsignor Thomas F. Cribbin (1917-2002) ministered to the Deaf community for sixty years.*

❖ *Anthonian Hall, Fort Greene, 1944.*

Schools offered workers courses on parliamentary procedure, labor law and Catholic social thought. By 1950, there were thirty labor schools throughout Long Island.

In the field of childcare, religious communities continued to exercise a prominent role. In 1937, the Marianist Brothers took over St. John's Home for Boys on Albany Avenue, which the Sisters of St. Joseph had directed since 1868. In 1948, the home was relocated to Rockaway Park. In 1930, Monsignor Bernard Quinn, the founding pastor of St. Peter Claver parish, founded the Little Flower House of Providence, an orphanage for African-American children, in Wading River. He faced fierce opposition from the Ku Klux Klan, which then had a substantial membership in Suffolk. The Sisters of the Blessed Sacrament, founded by St. Katherine Drexel in 1891, directed the home at its inception. They were succeeded by the Sisters of the Holy Family of Nazareth, a Polish community that also directed St. Peter Claver School.

Diocesan ministry to the elderly and handicapped continued to develop. The Little Sisters of the Poor operated three homes for the aged in Brooklyn and Queens. In 1934, Anthonian Hall, a home for blind women, opened in the former Chancery building. In 1936, as St. Joseph's School for the Deaf moved to the Bronx, Father George Haye was appointed to direct the newly formed Deaf Apostolate. His interest in deaf ministry began at the seminary in Huntington. Haye edited *Ephpheta*, the national Catholic magazine for the deaf. After he was ordained in 1942, Father (later Monsignor) Thomas Cribbin began a sixty-year ministry to the deaf. Over the years he became widely regarded as an authority on the pastoral care of the handicapped.

In 1931, Auxiliary Bishop Bernard J. Sheil of Chicago founded the Catholic

❖ *Legion of Decency Movie Ratings for 1936.*

Youth Organization (CYO). The most successful youth program in American Catholic history, the CYO sponsored summer camps, sports programs, and educational programs. Within a few years, dioceses throughout the nation established CYO programs. In 1940, Father Charles J. Bermingham started Brooklyn's CYO program, which expanded rapidly across Long Island. A hugely successful inter-parochial sports program was only one aspect of the many programs that Brooklyn's CYO sponsored. By 1952, it served 8,000 youth at four summer camps.

The bulk of Catholic Charities' financial support came from individuals and private organizations such as the Emerald Association and the Brooklyn Benevolent Society. New agencies such as the Italian Board of Guardians and the Ferrini Welfare League took a specific interest in the children of Italian immigrant families. Between 1929 and 1953, the Emerald Ball raised $541,000 for childcare on Long Island.

Patrick Scanlan and *The Tablet*

Under Patrick Scanlan's editorship, *The Tablet* became one of America's premier diocesan papers. Father James Hennesey writes that few papers "had the spice of the *Brooklyn Tablet*, edited by the redoubtable Patrick Scanlan." Over the years, Scanlan became known as the most vehement anticommunist in the American Catholic press, the foe of anti-Catholicism wherever he saw it, wary of ecumenism, and distrustful of expanded governmental power. For half a century, writes former *Tablet* editor Don Zirkel, "Pat Scanlan was *The Tablet*."

During the 1920's, one of Scanlan's major concerns was the rise of anti-Catholicism. The growth of the Klan became a frequent topic of his editorials as he urged Catholics to band together in

Archbishop Thomas E. Molloy (1922-1956)

❖ *The Mission of the Catholic Press, as seen in the pages of* The Tablet.

❖ *By the 1950's, Patrick F. Scanlan was known as the "Dean of the American Catholic Press."*

❖ *During the 1930's, the Spanish Civil War was a major concern for* The Tablet.

❖ *In the summer of 1923, Our Lady of Solace, Coney Island, was defaced by anti-Catholic bigots.*

❖ *Under Scanlan,* The Tablet *became the foremost anticommunist Catholic periodical in America.*

the defense of their common interests. During the 1928 presidential campaign, anti-Catholicism played a significant factor in the defeat of the Democratic candidate, Governor Alfred E. Smith of New York. The 1928 campaign confirmed Scanlan's belief that Catholics must remain militantly united against a hostile Protestant establishment. "Between the Church and a successful football team," he told

Tablet readers, "there is an analogy. Both have to fight."

By the 1930's, anti-Catholicism became less of a concern for Scanlan than the Great Depression. While he initially supported President Franklin D. Roosevelt's economic recovery program, he soon became disenchanted with what he considered an increase in

PATRICK F. SCANLAN (1894-1983)

Born in Manhattan, "Pat" Scanlan was one of seven children born to Michael and Maria O'Keefe Scanlan. Three of his brothers became priests of the Archdiocese of New York. After graduating from St. Joseph's College, Philadelphia, he briefly attended St. Joseph's Seminary, Dunwoodie, but he soon realized that his vocation was to serve the Church as a layman. In the fall of 1917, *The Tablet* hired Scanlan as a temporary managing editor to replace Joseph Cummings, who had joined the army. After Cummings died of influenza in 1918, Scanlan became permanent managing editor. An outspoken defender of the Church, he was known as a "one man anti-defamation league." His strong anticommunism brought national attention to the paper. His support of such controversial figures as Father Charles Coughlin and Senator Joseph McCarthy may have caused controversy, but no one questioned his loyalty to the Church. When Scanlan retired from the paper in October 1968, he retired to his home in Floral Park, where he lived until his death in 1983.

governmental bureaucracy and spending. Scanlan berated FDR's diplomatic recognition of Soviet Russia, and his inaction on Catholic persecutions in Mexico. By the late 1930's, Scanlan was the biggest supporter in the Catholic press of Father Charles Coughlin, the anti-Roosevelt "radio priest" whose anti-Semitic leanings aroused such controversy. Scanlan himself was not anti-Semitic, but he was critcal of what he considered Jewish insensitivity toward the persecution of the Church in nations such as Russia.

Brooklyn Catholics and World War II

As World War II approached, Scanlan strongly opposed American involvement. After Japanese planes attacked Pearl Harbor, however, he gave his full support to the war effort. *The Tablet* covered all aspects of the war from the

color-coded air raid signals that the Schools Office issued in 1943, to the stories of Catholic heroism on the battlefield. It is estimated that 214,000 Catholics from Long Island joined the military. Five thousand gave their lives in the struggle. During the war, 76 Brooklyn priests served as military chaplains. Father Lawrence Lynch, a Redemptorist who grew up in St. Sylvester's, City Line, was a Marine chaplain in the Pacific. In 1945, he was killed by a Japanese sniper at Okinawa as he was helping wounded troops.

On a Sunday morning in Bensonhurst, in May of 1942, the people of St. Rosalia's parish invoked Our Lady's intercession as they prayed for the safe return of American troops. They also vowed to build a shrine in her honor when

❖ *Air Raid signals are announced in this wartime* Tablet *issue.*

Archbishop Thomas E. Molloy (1922-1956)

❖ *Three McInenly brothers became Brooklyn priests. During World II, Father James (left) served as a U.S. Army Chaplain, and Father Joseph (right) in the U.S. Navy.*

❖ *Father Anthony De Laura, a U.S. Army Chaplain during World War II, blesses a wounded soldier.*

❖ *Seen here in this 1946 photo are a group of Brooklyn priests who served as chaplains in World War II.*

❖ *St. Rosalia-Regina Pacis, Bensonhurst.*

unimaginable opportunities awaited them in the form of the G.I. Bill, which President Roosevelt signed into law in June 1944. Returning veterans could attend college for free. The G.I. Bill, we will see, would have far-reaching effects on Catholic life.

Catholic Education

During his episcopate, Bishop Molloy erected over one hundred parochial schools, which had a student body of 175,000. For Molloy, Catholic education was not an exercise in sectarianism. By forming the nation's future leaders, he argued, all schools serve the common good, thereby rendering a valuable public service. In a 1939 pastoral letter, he wrote, "in reality there are no private institutions of public service." The Superintendent of Schools Office, under Monsignor Joseph V. McClancy and his successor Monsignor Henry M. Hald, centralized the diocesan school system through school

the war ended. In 1948, Monsignor Angelo R. Cioffi, the pastor, broke ground for the shrine. On August 15, 1951, the feast of the Assumption, Archbishop Molloy dedicated the Shrine Church of Regina Pacis ("Queen of Peace"). When the troops returned,

MONSIGNOR ANDREW P. LANDI (1906-1999)

❖ *Monsignor Andrew P. Landi is seen here with wartime refugees in Italy, 1945.*

Catholic Relief Services (CRS), now operating in over 90 countries, is the world's largest private relief organization. One of the leading figures in its early years was a Brooklyn priest who grew up in an orphanage in Bedford-Stuyvesant.

Baptized in Our Lady of Peace, Park Slope, Andrew Landi was one of six children. After his mother died when he was four, he was placed in St. John's Home, then located on Albany and St. Marks Avenues. After graduating from St. Francis College in 1930, he entered the newly-opened Seminary of the Immaculate Conception. He was part of the first ordination class in 1934.

Father Landi's first assignment was to St. Finbar, an Italian parish in Brooklyn's Bath Beach sec-

tion. When he was assigned there, however, he did not speak Italian. During the 1930's, he visited Italy and learned the language, an experience that would later serve him well. In 1939, he joined the staff of Catholic Charities as an assistant director.

In 1943, under the auspices of the National Catholic Welfare Conference, Catholic Relief Services was founded to meet the needs of Europe's wartime refugees. CRS needed priests who could speak Italian, and Father Landi joined its staff in 1944. He was sent to Italy, where he directed what was then the largest wartime relief project in history. In honor of his work, Pope Pius XII named him a Monsignor in 1945 (one of the youngest Brooklyn priests to be so honored).

After the war, Monsignor Landi stayed with CRS in Europe, directing resettlement work with displaced persons. In 1959, the Italian government awarded him the Star of Solidarity and the Order of Merit. In 1962, he was named regional director for CRS, overseeing relief work in Europe, North Africa and the Middle East. He returned to the United States in 1967, becoming CRS' assistant executive director. Even after he officially retired from the organization in 1979, Landi continued to serve as assistant treasurer until his death on September 8, 1999. Monsignor Landi's relief work, both during and after World War II, placed him in direct contact with Popes Pius XII, John XXIII, Paul VI and John Paul II.

visitations, curriculum reviews, and mandated quarterly reports.

By 1956, 28 communities of female religious, and seven male, were teaching in the Diocese. Some of the new communities included the Sisters of the Immaculate Heart of Mary who opened St. Ephrem's School in 1922. Over the next seven years, they opened six schools in the Diocese. The Dominican Sisters of Sparkill opened St. Edmund's School in 1923. By

1951, they had opened five parochial schools. In 1924, Sisters of Charity, Halifax, opened Our Lady of Angels School in Bay Ridge. Under Molloy they opened eleven schools. Older communities expanded their apostolate outside the Diocese, as in 1930 when the Josephites opened schools in Puerto Rico.

When Bishop Molloy took over the Diocese in 1922, there was a pressing need for new high schools. Over the next decade he opened Bishop McDonnell

Archbishop Thomas E. Molloy (1922-1956)

❖ *St. Edmund's School, Sheepshead Bay, 1927.*

❖ *St. Ephrem School, Dyker Heights, 1923.*

❖ *Students at Our Lady of Grace, Howard Beach, 1928.*

❖ *First Graders, Holy Child Jesus, Richmond Hill, 1924*

Memorial High School, St. Brendan, St. Barbara, St. Edmund and St. Michael (now Xaverian). In 1933, Bishop Loughlin Memorial High School opened on the site of the unfinished Cathedral of the Immaculate Conception. Between 1936 and 1943, the Josephites opened three girls' high schools: The Mary Louis Academy, Fontbonne Hall Academy and Stella Maris High School. In 1936, the Dominicans opened Dominican Commercial High School in Jamaica. In 1955, the Holy Cross Brothers opened Holy Cross High School, the first Catholic boys' high school in Queens County. In 1956, the Brothers of the Sacred Heart opened Monsignor McClancy Memorial High School in East Elmhurst. By then, Long Island had 55 Catholic high schools, with a student population of 74,000.

As large as his school system was, Bishop Molloy realized that there was an equally large number of Catholic children who did not attend parochial school. By the 1930's, there were over 100,000 Catholic children attending public schools. In 1936, therefore, he directed every parish in the Diocese to establish a Confraternity of Christian Doctrine (CCD) program.

Catholic higher education made significant advances during the Molloy years. During the 1920's, St. Francis College and St. Joseph's both

❖ *Monsignor Henry M. Hald (1893-1966)*

❖ *St. Anselm, Bay Ridge, 1943.*

❖ *Eighth Graders, St. Andrew Avellino, Flushing, 1951.*

❖ *In 1933, the Christian Brothers closed St. James Academy and opened Bishop Loughlin Memorial High School in Fort Greene.*

❖ *Bishop McDonnell Memorial High School. Closed in 1973, the building now houses St. Frances de Sales School for the Deaf.*

❖ *Students at Nativity of the Blessed Virgin Mary School, Ozone Park, ca. 1930*

expanded their facilities. In 1933, St. John's College in Brooklyn officially changed its name to St. John's University. St. John's opened a law school in 1925, a downtown campus in 1927, and a pharmacy school in 1929. In 1954, the university moved from Bedford-Stuyvesant to its new Queens campus, which had

SISTERS OF THE CATHOLIC APOSTOLATE (PALLOTTINES)

Founded in Italy in 1835 by St. Vincent Pallotti, this women's religious community has worked in the Brooklyn Diocese for over 80 years. In 1922, the Sisters began an outreach to Brooklyn's growing Italian community, at St. Lucy's parish in Fort Greene. At the St. Thomas Settlement House on Kent Avenue, they helped Italian immigrants adjust to American life. During the 1930's, they expanded their apostolate to St. Fortunata's, East New York, conducting catechetical and census work in a heavily Italian neighborhood. In 1935, they were invited to Our Lady of Grace in Gravesend, and to St. Finbar, Bath Beach, in 1940. During the 1940's, the Sisters worked briefly at St. Louis parish, which closed in 1946.

In 1948, the Sisters moved into Queens, where Msgr. Leopoldo Arcese invited them to work at Nativity of the Blessed Virgin Mary in Ozone Park. In 1952, the Sisters entered the classroom for the first time when they took over Our Lady of Grace School, Gravesend. In 1957, they took charge of St. Fortunata's School, and St. Finbar School in 1963. From 1959 to 1971, the Sisters ran St. Stephen's High School, Carroll Gardens. Today they continue their work at St. Finbar's School, preserving a long tradition of service to Brooklyn's immigrants.

---

formerly been a golf course. In 1955, the Dominican Sisters opened Molloy College in Rockville Centre, the second Catholic women's college on Long Island.

Evangelization and Outreach

During Bishop Molloy's episcopate, a significant outreach to non-Catholics had developed. In 1938, Molloy founded the Brooklyn Diocesan Apostolate for the Instruction of Non-Catholics, the first official diocesan effort of its kind in America. Each January a five-week course of instruction in the faith began at fifty locations throughout the Diocese. The Diocesan League of Converts was open to converts wishing to become more familiar with particular Catholic issues and questions. In 1953, after Pope Pius XII hailed the radio as a means for promoting Christian formation, Archbishop Molloy committed the Diocese to using the local airwaves, such as WWRL in Woodside (and others), to broadcast religious educational programs.

A significant outreach was developed for Catholics as well. At Brooklyn's Precious Blood Monastery, the chaplains, Monsignor Joseph F. Stedman and his successor, Monsignor Joseph Frey, promoted the Confraternity of the Precious Blood. Stedman and Frey wrote and edited missals and prayer books which were distributed to American troops during World War II, and which were translated into almost a dozen languages. *My Daily Bread*, by Jesuit Father Anthony Paone, continues to be a bestseller. The Cana Conferences for married couples, begun in Chicago, came to the Diocese in 1946. The Newman Apostolate, begun in 1883 as an outreach to Catholic students attending non-Catholic colleges and

❖ *Italian Eucharistic Congress, Bensonhurst, 1961.*

❖ *Knights of Columbus at One Prospect Park West, 1925.*

750,000 that they reflected "the inner spirit of unity that has made America strong." Each year in Brooklyn on Memorial Day, the Knights of Columbus Field Mass at the Parade Grounds drew an average of 75,000 people.

Devotional societies abounded during this period, especially those fostering eucharistic devotion. The Nocturnal Adoration Society, a Catholic men's group that organized nightly vigils before the Blessed Sacrament, was founded in Italy in 1809. American branches were founded in Boston and Baltimore in 1882. Monsignor Charles Vitta, the pastor of Holy Name, Park Slope, established a Brooklyn branch in 1930. Each member was required to offer one hour a month in prayer before the tabernacle, a "Holy Hour." By 1953, it had 3,500 members throughout the Diocese. In 1952, a Women's Eucharistic Crusade was established for the same purpose. The Family Communion Crusade, founded in 1950, encouraged families to receive communion together at least once a month, and encouraged devotion to the Holy Family.

In 1935, Father Edward J. Higgins, the pastor of Immaculate Conception parish in Astoria, founded the Catholic War Veterans (CWV). Higgins, who had been an army chaplain in World War I, envisioned the CWV as a Catholic counterpart to the American Legion. After World War II, it became one of the nation's most influential patriotic organizations. During the early Cold War, the CWV promoted veterans' issues while leading the fight against Communism. By 1947, its membership was nearly 500,000 nationwide. In 1944 Ruth Manning was elected as the national Vice-Commander, the first woman to be elected to the national board of a veterans' organization.

The Knights of Columbus expanded significantly during this period. By the 1950's, there were 75 councils on Long

❖ *Middle:* The Tablet *advertises Forty Hours devotions, 1948.*
❖ *Left: A group of prominent Italian pastors plan the 1953 Italian Eucharistic Congress.*
❖ *Right:* The Tablet *urges men to get involved in their parish Holy Name Society.*

Archbishop Thomas E. Molloy (1922-1956)

❖ *The Boys Choir of Blessed Sacrament, Cypress Hills, during the 1940's.*

❖ *In 1935, Monsignor Edward J. Higgins founded the Catholic War Veterans at Immaculate Conception, Long Island City.*

❖*The 1949 Loyalty Day Parade made* The Tablet's *front page news.*

❖*The altar, Immaculate Conception, Long Island City (1924).*

❖ The Tablet *advertises a Knights of Columbus-sponsored rodeo in Brooklyn.*

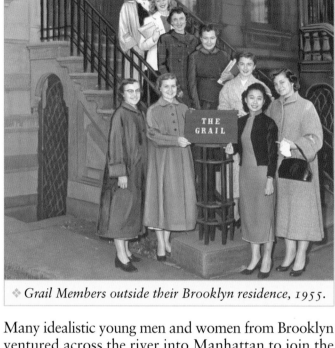

❖ *Grail Members outside their Brooklyn residence, 1955.*

Island, with a total membership of 30,000. In November 1925, Columbus Council No. 126 opened at Brooklyn's Grand Army Plaza. This impressive edifice soon became a center for Brooklyn Catholic life. The Columbus Council Forum featured nationally renowned speakers such as Bishop Fulton J. Sheen and Father John LaFarge, S.J., editor of *America* magazine. Its Institute of Modern Thought offered lecture series on a variety of topics, including Catholic social thought, literature, philosophy and history. Scholarships, blood drives, shelter homes, and public awareness campaigns were only some of the Knights' activities.

On the eve of World War II, it is estimated that there were over 250 Catholic women's organizations on Long Island. These included the Legion of Mary, the Catholic Daughters of the Americas, and the International Federation of Catholic Alumnae. In 1941, the Diocesan Council of Catholic Women was formed to coordinate their activities. The Grail movement, a lay movement introduced from Holland in the 1940's, emphasized young Catholic women's potential to change the world. Grail spirituality stressed the connection between an active participation in the liturgy and social reform. In 1947, its Brooklyn center opened, which sponsored programs on the arts and liturgy. During the 1950's, members of the Brooklyn Grail organized credit unions and cooperatives in Brooklyn's poor neighborhoods.

❖ *Dorothy Day (1897-1980)*

Many idealistic young men and women from Brooklyn ventured across the river into Manhattan to join the Catholic Worker movement. The *Catholic Worker*, started by Peter Maurin and the Brooklyn-born Dorothy Day, offered a program of radical evangelical poverty hitherto unseen in American Catholic life. Through their newspaper *The Catholic Worker* and their "Houses of Hospitality," Day and Maurin translated the Gospel mandate into a radical identification with the urban poor and destitute.

Beginning in the 1940's, Brooklyn Catholics took an active role in the growing civil rights movement. In May 1934, Father John LaFarge, S.J., formed the Catholic Interracial Council of New York, the purpose of which was to promote interracial harmony and advance the cause of racial equality. In April 1944, Monsignor Raymond Campion, the pastor of St. Peter Claver, Bedford-Stuyvesant, founded a Brooklyn branch. Some of the council's Brooklyn activities included a speakers' bureau, radio broadcasts, communion breakfasts and exhibits. Monsignor Archibald V. McLees, who was named moderator in 1951, became a leading Catholic supporter of the Civil Rights Movement.

During Bishop Molloy's time, retreats for the laity became increasingly popular. In

Archbishop Thomas E. Molloy (1922-1956)

❖ *Archbishop Molloy with members of the Catholic Interracial Council, 1954.*

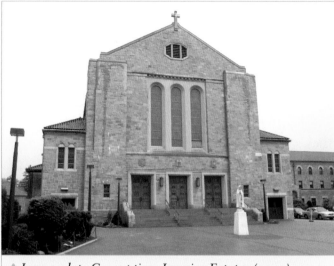

❖ *Immaculate Conception, Jamaica Estates (1924)*

1921, the Religious of the Cenacle opened a retreat house in Lake Ronkonkoma. In its first 25 years, 50,000 women visited the house. Beginning in 1930, the Passionists offered retreats for men at Bishop Molloy Retreat House in Jamaica Estates. By 1953, over 5,000 men a year were passing through its doors. In 1949, the Dominicans opened a women's retreat house at their new motherhouse in Amityville, and the Religious of the Sacred Heart of Mary opened another in Sag Harbor. In 1953, the Pallottine Fathers opened a retreat house for men in North Haven.

During the summer months, many Brooklyn Catholics spent their vacations at the Catholic Summer Camp in Cliff Haven, New York. Cliff Haven, a 400-acre facility along the shores of Lake Champlain, offered a setting for Catholic families to relax, and courses in spiritual and cultural enrichment. Sports programs, daily Mass, and musical concerts were also part of its daily schedule. In 1941, Archbishop Francis J. Spellman of New York presided over the camp's golden jubilee celebration.

Brooklyn Catholics and the Missions

One striking indication of Diocesan growth under Molloy was its contribution to the foreign missions. When the Diocese was erected in 1853, it was essentially a missionary endeavor. During its early years, the Society of the Propagation of the Faith provided much needed financial support. Later on in 1904, Bishop McDonnell founded the Society's

Brooklyn branch under Msgr. James S. Duffy, the pastor of St. Agnes in Carroll Gardens. During the first thirty years of Bishop Molloy's episcopate, Brooklyn Catholics contributed over $15,000,000 to the foreign missions. By the 1950's, Mission Sunday in October was a major event in parishes, celebrated with elaborate preparation and pomp as school children dressed up as priests, nuns, brothers, bishops, and even pope.

Brooklyn Catholics also gave to the missions in other ways. By 1953, Brooklyn had given more vocations to Maryknoll than any other diocese, nearly twelve percent of the order's personnel. Father Francis X. Ford, a native of St. Joseph in Prospect Heights, was one of Maryknoll's first missionaries to China. Ordained a bishop in 1935, he died in a Chinese communist prison in 1952. In 1912, Father Edward Galvin left Holy Rosary parish in Bedford-Stuyvesant for the Chinese missions. He founded the Columban Fathers in 1918; in 1927 he was ordained a Bishop in China. In 1952, the communist regime expelled him. In 1945, Father Apollinaris Baumgartner, a Capuchin who grew up in College Point, was consecrated Vicar Apostolic of Guam. Father James E. McManus, a Redemptorist from Bay Ridge, was consecrated Bishop of Ponce, Puerto Rico, in 1947.

Archbishop Molloy and the Diocesan Centennial

In 1953, the Diocese of Brooklyn turned 100, and Brooklyn Catholics had much to celebrate. In the space of a century, their numbers had gone from

Archbishop Thomas E. Molloy (1922-1956)

❖ *Mission Sunday, St. Michael, Flushing, during the 1950's.*

❖ *Left: Bishop James E. McManus, C.Ss.R. (1900-1976). A Bay Ridge native, in 1947 he was named Bishop of Ponce, Puerto Rico.*
❖ *Right: Bishop Francis X. Ford, M.M., (1892-1952), was baptized in Sacred Heart, Fort Greene, and grew up in St. Joseph's, Prospect Heights.*

15,000 to 1.4 million. The number of parishes rose from 15 to 347. Brooklyn was the largest diocese in the United States. By then it had more Catholics than the Archdiocese of New York. Only the Archdiocese of Chicago had a larger Catholic population.

By 1953, Brooklyn had nearly 1,200 diocesan priests, compared to 587 when Bishop McDonnell died. (Between 1930 and 1960, the Diocese ordained an average of 35 priests a year.) Over 4,000 male and female religious ministered throughout the Diocese. Rumors abounded that Brooklyn would be raised to an Archdiocese. Although that never happened, in April 1951 Pope Pius XII named Molloy an Archbishop *ad personam*, a personal title that honored his years of outstanding leadership.

On January 12, 1953, at St. James Cathedral, Archbishop Amleto Cicognani, the Apostolic Delegate to the United States, celebrated a Pontifical Mass to inaugurate the centennial observance. In his sermon, Auxiliary Bishop Raymond A. Kearney, the Chancellor, paid tribute to Long Island's Catholic pioneers. The foreword to *The Tablet*'s

❖ *Program for the Diocese's Centennial Mass, 1953.*

commemorative centennial issue expressed Brooklyn Catholic confidence in the future:

Looking ahead, humbly we can hope that future generations will find in our words and works the same admiration and pride that we today possess for the faith, the virtue, and the self-sacrifice of those who have gone before us. In this humble spirit, invoking the blessing of Almighty God and the protection of our Patroness, Mary, the Immaculate Mother of God, we rejoice in the accomplishments of the past and address ourselves to the tasks of the future.

Bishop Kearney became Molloy's first Auxiliary Bishop in 1935. In Molloy's later years, as his health declined, he had new Auxiliaries to help him. In June 1952, Monsignor John J. Boardman, Director of the Society for the Propagation of the Faith, was consecrated at Our Lady of Perpetual Help in Bay Ridge. Monsignor Edmund J. Reilly, Pastor of Our Lady of Angels, Bay Ridge, was named an Auxiliary Bishop in 1955. In 1956, Monsignor John J. Carberry was appointed Bishop of Lafayette,

Archbishop Thomas E. Molloy (1922-1956)

❖ *Archbishop Molloy with Auxiliary Bishops Raymond A. Kearney, Edmund J. Reilly and John J. Boardman, 1955.*

❖ *Ordained in 1929, John J. Carberry (center) became Coadjutor Bishop of Lafayette in 1956. In 1969 he became the second Brooklyn priest to be created a Cardinal.*

❖ The Tablet *commemorates the Diocese's Centennial, 1953.*

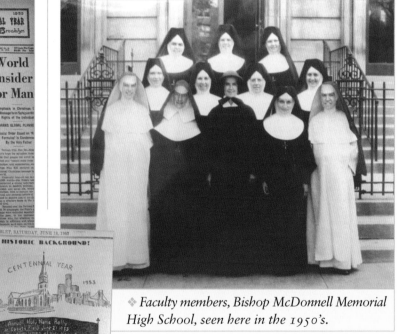

❖ *Faculty members, Bishop McDonnell Memorial High School, seen here in the 1950's.*

Indiana. He later became Archbishop of St. Louis, and in 1969 he was named a Cardinal.

On November 26, 1956, Archbishop-Bishop Thomas E. Molloy died of a stroke at age 71. He was buried (with a copy of *The Tablet*) alongside his predecessors at the seminary he had founded. Over the years, rumors abounded that Molloy would be transferred to an archdiocese, but it was said that he refused to leave Brooklyn. Patrick Scanlan recalled that Molloy once told him: "When I die, I hope that heaven is a lot like Brooklyn."

❖ *During the Diocesan Centennial celebration, the Holy Name Society sponsored a mega-rally at Ebbets Field.*

CHAPTER FIVE

The Winds of Change:
Archbishop Bryan J. McEntegart
(1957-1968)

Church and Nation in the Sixties

❖ *Vatican II in session.*

In 1960, America faced the future with an enthusiastic vigor, confident in its ability to better both the nation and the world. A young and enthusiastic President John F. Kennedy, embodied this optimism, calling for a "new generation" of Americans to pick up the torch of liberty handed down to them by their forefathers. Idealistic young men and women responded to the challenge by joining the Peace Corps, by journeying South to join the Civil Rights movement, and by joining the war on domestic poverty. In his brief tenure, JFK struck a chord of altruism among American youth that set a keynote for the sixties.

For American Catholics, the 1960's was an exciting time. The election of a Roman Catholic to the presidency was a "coming of age experience" for American Catholics. In Rome, a new pope, John XXIII, made preparations for an ecumenical council whose goal was to address the Church's relationship to the modern world. Professor David O'Brien, who graduated from the University of Notre Dame in 1960, writes that Pope John XXIII and President John F. Kennedy were the "two idols of my generation."

In the fields of science and technology, the sixties saw rapid advances, most especially as it applied to space exploration. Scientific advances created a sense of optimism about the future, a belief that Americans could overcome any obstacle, conquer any frontier. These advances were well displayed at the 1964 World's Fair, which was held at Corona-Flushing

Archbishop Bryan J. McEntegart (1957-1968)

❖ *President John F. Kennedy (1917-1963)*

❖ *At St. James Cathedral, Monsignor Francis J. Mugavero presides at a Memorial Mass for President John F. Kennedy, November 1963.*

❖ *Pope Blessed John XXIII convenes Vatican II, October 11, 1962.*

❖ *Aerial view of the World's Fair, 1964-1965.*

Meadow Park in Queens. By the end of the decade, an American astronaut, Neil Armstrong, became the first human being to walk on the moon.

As the Sixties progressed, however, its early optimism wavered in the face of political and cultural disintegration. America's commitment to halt the spread of communism led to a ten-year conflict in Vietnam, in which 55,000 American troops were killed. Antiwar protests spread throughout the country. JFK's assassination, increased racial tension, and urban decay would all contribute to a loss of hope, a sense of lost innocence in society at large.

The tensions of the Sixties were heightened for American Catholics, as they deliberated over how to implement the decrees of the Second Vatican Council (1962-1965). They tried to discern how the Church should properly address the major political, social and economic issues of the day in light of the council's teaching. Under the leadership of a new Bishop,

Archbishop Bryan J. McEntegart (1957-1968)

❖ *Bishop McEntegart's installation Mass at Our Lady of Perpetual Help, Bay Ridge.*

❖ *Cardinal Francis J. Spellman and Bishop McEntegart at the installation Mass.*

Brooklyn Catholics faced the challenges and changes of the Sixties in a spirit of *aggiornamento* as they attempted to implement the council in a diocese whose size had shrunk but whose demands had increased.

1957: A New Diocese, A New Bishop

For Brooklynites, the year 1957 was a significant one, as Walter O'Malley announced that the Dodgers would leave Brooklyn for Los Angeles. That year was especially significant for Brooklyn Catholics as well. After the death of Archbishop Molloy in November 1956, Msgr. Edward P. Hoar, the Vicar General, served as temporary Diocesan Administrator. On Holy Thursday, April 16, 1957, Archbishop Amleto Cicognani, the Apostolic Delegate to the United States, announced that Pope Pius XII had created a new diocese out of Nassau and Suffolk Counties, the Diocese of Rockville Centre. It was also announced that Bishop Bryan J. McEntegart, Rector of The Catholic University of America, had been named the fourth Bishop of Brooklyn.

By the end of Archbishop Molloy's episcopate, it was clear that the Church on Long Island would be better served if a separate diocese were created for Nassau and Suffolk

Counties. During the 1950's, Suffolk experienced a population increase of ninety percent, while Nassau was the fastest growing county in the United States. As their Catholic population grew rapidly, Rome decided that it was time to erect a new diocese. Bishop Walter P. Kellenberg was named the first Bishop of Rockville Centre. Ordained a priest of the Archdiocese of New York in 1928, Kellenberg succeeded McEntegart as Bishop of Ogdensburg in 1954.

On June 13, 1957, at Our Lady of Perpetual Help in Bay Ridge, Bishop Bryan J. McEntegart took canonical possession of the Diocese of Brooklyn, now consisting of Kings and Queens Counties. Geographically, Brooklyn would now be the smallest diocese in the United States, at 179 square miles. In terms of its population, however, it would remain the largest. Among the

SALUS ANIMARUM SUPREMA LEX

❖ *Archbishop McEntegart's episcopal coat of arms*

Archbishop Bryan J. McEntegart (1957-1968)

❖ *Our Lady of the Cenacle, Richmond Hill (1922)*

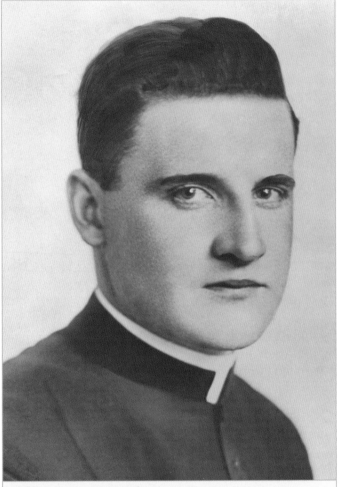

❖ *The newly ordained Father McEntegart, September 1917.*

archdioceses, only New York, Chicago and Boston had a larger number of Catholics. As a result of the erection of the Diocese of Rockville Centre, Brooklyn became the only completely *urban* diocese in the United States.

Bishop Bryan J. McEntegart

The son of Irish immigrants, Bryan Joseph McEntegart was born in Manhattan in 1893. After graduating from Manhattan College in 1913, McEntegart studied at St. Joseph's Seminary, Dunwoodie. In 1917, at St. Patrick's Cathedral, he was ordained a priest of the Archdiocese of New York. As a young priest, McEntegart became interested in the pastoral care of children and the elderly. After earning a degree in social work at The Catholic University of America, he served for two decades as director of childcare for Catholic Charities in the archdiocese, becoming a nationally renowned expert on this issue.

During the early 1940's, McEntegart was instrumental in the formation of the NCWC's War Relief Services. Renamed Catholic Relief Services, the organization is the largest voluntary welfare agency of its kind in history. In 1943, he was named Bishop of Ogdensburg, New York, where he remained until he was named Rector of Catholic University in 1953. McEntegart's experience in pastoral care, social work and education made him well qualified to meet the needs of a changing city.

The Changing Face of the City

In 1964, at Corona-Flushing Meadow Park, the Unisphere, a stainless steel model of the globe, was erected as the symbol of the World's Fair. In a way, the Unisphere can also be seen as a symbol of the Brooklyn Catholic experience. At one time or another, people from every region of the world have either passed through Brooklyn or made it their home. The

Archbishop Bryan J. McEntegart (1957-1968)

❖ *Monsignor McEntegart with former New York Governor Alfred E. Smith (right), ca. 1941.*

❖ *La Sociedad del Santo Nombre, St. Peter-Our Lady of Pilar, 1959.*

❖ *Stained glass window, St. Clare, Rosedale (1924).*

Unisphere reminds us of the Church's uniquely immigrant character in Brooklyn and Queens. It might also invite Brooklyn Catholics to reflect on the Church's presence in an ever-changing modern world.

Bishop McEntegart came to Brooklyn at a time when New York City was undergoing major demographic shifts. From 1940 to 1970, as many blacks left the South for a better life, the city's African-American population grew from 450,000 to 1.7 million. During the 1940's, and again in the 1960's, New York experienced a

❖ *The Tablet lists Brooklyn and Queens parishes providing services for the Spanish-speaking, 1958.*

wave of Puerto Rican migration. By 1958 Brooklyn's Puerto Rican population was nearly 200,000. Immigrants from Cuba, the Dominican Republic, Haiti and Jamaica also began to make their presence felt in city life.

Such demographic changes affected parishes in Brooklyn and Queens. Neighborhoods that had been predominantly white ethnic European now experienced an influx of Hispanic, Caribbean and African-American residents. In some cases, parishes experienced a serious decline when the neighborhood became

Archbishop Bryan J. McEntegart (1957-1968)

❖ *The Unisphere, Corona-Flushing Meadow Park.*

❖ *La Fiesta de San Juan Bautista is celebrated at Visitation, Red Hook, 1962.*

predominantly non-Catholic. In many cases, parishes with a traditionally Irish congregation now had a predominantly Hispanic one. In 1958, only twelve parishes in the Diocese offered Mass in Spanish, but that number would grow rapidly over the next ten years.

During the 1960's, St. Mary Star of the Sea in Far Rockaway began to regularly celebrate *La Fiesta de la Nuestra Senora de la Caridad del Cobre*, the Patroness of Cuba. The feast day was celebrated at a Mass with a sermon in Spanish, followed by a procession of the statue of Our Lady and Benediction of the Blessed Sacrament. June 24, the feast of San Juan Bautista, is an integral part of Puerto Rican culture. At St. John the Baptist in Bedford-Stuyvesant, the Vincentians celebrated the day with a Mass followed by festivities across the street from the church on Carey Field.

During the early 1960's, Brooklyn neighborhoods such as Williamsburg, Brownsville, Fort Greene and Bushwick had developed substantial Hispanic communities. In response, Bishop McEntegart formulated a comprehensive outreach to serve the needs of Hispanic-Latino communities throughout the Brooklyn Diocese. McEntegart himself took a three-month Spanish course in Puerto Rico. Aside from several Redemptorists and Vincentians, however, there were few Spanish-speaking priests in the Diocese when he arrived. In 1958, he began assigning newly ordained priests to study Spanish at The Catholic University of Ponce in Puerto Rico, which would also offer an opportunity for cultural immersion. During the 1960's, nearly 300 priests, religious and laypeople studied in Ponce.

Some of the young priests that McEntegart assigned to Ponce, such as Monsignors John Peyton and John Powis, have been active in East New York and Bushwick's Hispanic communities for nearly five decades. Monsignor Bryan Karvelis, ordained in 1956, has spent his entire priesthood at Transfiguration

❖ *Our Lady of Refuge, Flatbush (1911)*

Archbishop Bryan J. McEntegart (1957-1968)

❖ *Students at Ponce, Puerto Rico, August 1967.*

❖ *Father Lawrence Hinch, Director of the St. Paul Center, celebrates Mass at a women's retreat, 1967.*

❖ *Born in Spain, Vincentian Father Jaime Pico ministered to Brooklyn's Hispanic Catholics for nearly half a century.*

❖ *Dedication of Our Lady of Montserrate Chapel, Bedford-Stuyvesant.*

ministering to Hispanics in Williamsburg. For over forty years, Monsignor Matthew Foley (a classmate of Msgr. Karvelis) has served the people of nearby Epiphany parish.

Hispanic Catholics made an important impression on the life of the Church in America, and especially in Brooklyn, through the Cursillo movement. A retreat movement founded in Spain in the 1950's, the Cursillo first came to Brooklyn in 1962. In 1963, the St. Peter's Cursillo Center opened in what had been the nursing residence for St. Peter's Hospital (which closed in 1962). By 1967, nearly 5,000 Spanish-speaking Catholics had participated in the Cursillo. In 1966, Father Lawrence Hinch became the first director of the St. Paul Center, which continues to offer a Cursillo experience to English-speaking Catholics.

Under McEntegart, over fifty parishes in Brooklyn and Queens had developed a significant Hispanic outreach. The services they offered included job placement, housing assistance, immigration questions,

and care for the elderly. Catholic Charities sponsored local self-help projects such as *Arriba Juntos* ("Forward Together") in Williamsburg; these, together with the growing Cursillo movement, allowed

Archbishop Bryan J. McEntegart (1957-1968)

❖ *Transfiguration, Williamsburg (1874)*

❖ *The Bishops enter St. Peter's Basilica for the council, 1962.*

❖ *Bishop McEntegart at the council, along with Auxiliary Bishops John J. Boardman, Charles R. Mulrooney, and Joseph P. Denning.*

Brooklyn's Hispanic community to maintain its religious and cultural identity while developing leadership roles for youth. For McEntegart, the growth of Hispanic culture in New York, with its deeply Catholic roots, could serve as an important antidote to a growing secularism and materialism in the larger society.

Vatican II (1962-1965)

On October 28, 1958, the Cardinal-Patriarch of Venice, Angelo Giuseppe Roncalli, was elected pope. A former Church History professor and career diplomat, he took the name John XXIII. On January 25, 1959, Pope John announced a synod for the Diocese of Rome and an ecumenical council for the universal church. He also announced his intention to revise the Code of Canon Law. For John, the goal of the council was clear. While remaining faithful to Catholic doctrine, it sought to respond to the signs of the times.

From its opening on October 11, 1962, the Second Vatican Council's progress received worldwide media coverage. Both the secular and the Catholic press covered the conciliar debates over the Church's relationship with the world and the calls for internal renewal. By the time of its closing on December 8, 1965, the council had published 16 documents whose aim was to identify and to articulate the Church's

Archbishop Bryan J. McEntegart (1957-1968)

❖ *The Pietá arrives in New York for the World's Fair, 1964.*

❖ *At the Vatican Pavilion, Pope Paul VI is accompanied by Monsignor Mugavero.*

❖ *St. Frances Cabrini, Bensonhurst (1963)*

met regularly while in Rome to discuss the issues. Several laypersons and a religious sister had been named as official observers. *Dignitatis Humanae*, the Declaration on Religious Liberty (December 7, 1965), was of particular pride for American Catholics, since the American *periti* played an active and instrumental role in drafting it. Bishop McEntegart and his three auxiliary bishops, John J. Boardman, Charles R. Mulrooney and Joseph P. Denning, were present at the council's sessions. They observed the conciliar debates, the death of John XXIII in 1963, and Pope Paul VI's commitment to continue what Pope John had begun.

In 1964, while the council fathers debated, the World's Fair was held in Flushing Meadow Park. At the request of the late Pope John XXIII, the Holy See was represented by the Vatican Pavilion. Bishop McEntegart served as the Vice President of the U.S.

nature and its redemptive mission in the world. The two major conciliar documents that addressed these issues were *Lumen Gentium*, the Dogmatic Constitution on the Church (November 21, 1964) and *Gaudium et Spes*, the Pastoral Constitution on the Church in the Modern World (December 7, 1965).

American participation at the council was strong, as bishops and their expert advisors, known as *periti*,

Archbishop Bryan J. McEntegart (1957-1968)

❖ *Seen here in this stained glass window flanking Christ are Pope Paul VI and Bishop McEntegart. This window is in the sacristy of St. Thomas Apostle, Woodhaven.*

Bishops' Committee for the Vatican Pavilion. One of its prime attractions was Michelangelo's *Pietá*, which the Holy See had lent to the pavilion for this occasion. (Approximately 27 million people visited the pavilion.) In April, Cardinal Paolo Marella, President of the Pontifical Council for Interreligious Dialogue, presided

at the dedication ceremony for the pavilion's Good Shepherd Chapel. In his homily, McEntegart drew a parallel between the Statue of Liberty, which symbolized American freedom, and the *Pietá*, which symbolized the Church's mission to promote true peace, the fruit of justice, in the world.

Nowhere was the Church's commitment to peace more dramatically presented than when Paul VI visited

Archbishop Bryan J. McEntegart (1957-1968)

❖ *Bishop McEntegart speaks at the Vatican Pavilion.*

❖ *Our Lady of Mercy, Brownsville (1961)*

the United Nations' General Assembly on October 4, 1965. "No more war," he poignantly shouted in his address to the assembly. "War never again!" Paul's journey to America was an unprecedented event in world history, the first time a pontiff had visited America. His first stop was in the Diocese of Brooklyn, when his plane arrived in John F. Kennedy International Airport. As a result, Bishop McEntegart became the first diocesan ordinary in the western hemisphere to welcome the Pope to his diocese.

Catholic Education

Coming from Catholic University to Brooklyn, it was natural that one of the new bishop's priorities should be education. The most immediate educational need that McEntegart faced was for more high schools. Bishop Molloy had created several new high schools in the 1920's, but by the 1950's a growing Catholic population warranted the creation of still more. In 1958, McEntegart commissioned a survey to investigate this issue, and in 1959 he made known his plans to expand the high school system.

In 1960, McEntegart announced his plans for a Diocesan Campaign, a fundraising drive for the new schools. The goal of the campaign was twenty million dollars. The Diocesan Campaign went far beyond anyone's expectations, raising a total of nearly $37 million. As a result of the campaign, three new high schools were built in Brooklyn, and three in Queens. The Brooklyn schools were Nazareth in East Flatbush, Bishop Kearney in Bensonhurst, and Bishop Ford in

Park Slope. In Queens, the schools established were Christ the King in Middle Village, Bishop Reilly (now St. Francis Preparatory School) in Fresh Meadows, and Mater Christi (now St. John's Preparatory School) in Astoria. Between 1957 and 1968, the enrollment in diocesan and parochial high schools would rise from 11,563 to 22,867.

As former rector of the nation's pontifical university, it was only natural that McEntegart took a close interest in Catholic higher education. In 1958, he presided at a dedication ceremony on St. John's University's new Queens campus. By 1963, student enrollment at the university passed twelve thousand, making it the nation's largest Catholic university. In 1960, St. Francis College moved from its home on Butler Street to Brooklyn Heights. St. Joseph's College took great pride in its outstanding early childhood development program. As Catholic students attended secular colleges and universities in greater numbers, McEntegart wanted to ensure that they had a place to integrate their studies and their faith. In 1963, the Newman Center opened its own building at Brooklyn College, while at the same time the campus outreach at Queens College was also expanded.

In the middle of the council, the Diocese played host to a significant gathering of international Catholic biblical scholars. In the summer of 1964, Queens served as the site for the 27th annual meeting of the Catholic Biblical Assocation. The convention, which drew over 150 biblical scholars from throughout the world, opened with a Mass at the Vatican Pavilion

Archbishop Bryan J. McEntegart (1957-1968)

❖ *Advertisement for the 1960 Diocesan Campaign.*

❖ *Our Lady of Consolation, Williamsburg, 1960.*

❖*Students at Archbishop Molloy High School during the 1960's.*

❖ *Brooklyn Preparatory School, 1965.*

❖ *During St. Joseph College's Fiftieth Anniversary in 1966, Archbishop McEntegart greets the school's first graduate.*

❖ *Cathedral College celebrates its Golden Jubilee Mass at St. Joseph, Pacific Street, 1965.*

Archbishop Bryan J. McEntegart (1957-1968)

❖ *Monsignor Eugene J. Molloy with Bishop McEntegart at Bishop Kearney High School, 1965.*

❖ *St. John's University, Queens Campus.*

❖ *St. Francis College at its new location on Remsen Street, Brooklyn Heights.*

❖ *Newman Center, Brooklyn College, 1964.*

celebrated by Auxiliary Bishop Charles R. Mulrooney. The meeting sessions took place in Jamaica Estates at Bishop Molloy Retreat House and The Mary Louis Academy. Father Roland de Vaux, O.P., the Director of the Ecole Biblique in Jerusalem, was one of the featured speakers.

As the council fathers debated in Rome, the council's progress was a source of much local interest. In the pages of *The Tablet*, the details of the debates were discussed for its readers. Local parishes sponsored lectures and evening courses that kept their parishioners informed about the issues being addressed at the council: the relationship between Church and State, the laity, ecumenism, the meaning of religious freedom, religious education, social justice, and the liturgy. At

Archbishop Bryan J. McEntegart (1957-1968)

❖ *Newman Center, Queens College, 1965.*

❖ *Dedication of Cathedral Preparatory Seminary, Elmhurst, 1963.*

❖ *Ordination Mass, St. James Cathedral, 1965.*

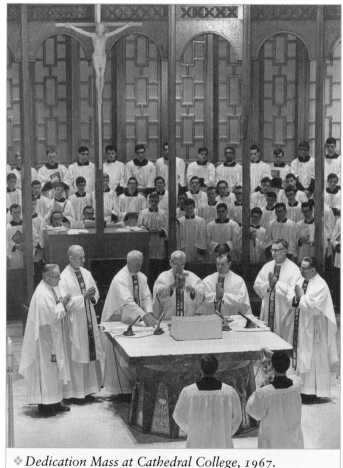

❖ *Dedication Mass at Cathedral College, 1967.*

Sunday Mass, parish priests used the pulpit as an opportunity to update the faithful on conciliar issues.

The Changing Face of the Priesthood

As the number of priestly vocations continued to grow, McEntegart decided that the time had come to expand the seminary system. Between 1930 and 1960, an average of 35 men a year were ordained to the priesthood. By the early 1960's, the facilities at Cathedral College, located at the corner of Washington and Atlantic Avenues in Brooklyn, were proving inadequate to the needs of a growing student body. As a result, a number of classes were held at nearby St. Joseph's parochial school.

In 1963, a second preparatory seminary was opened in Queens. High school-age young men in that borough, who were discerning a priestly vocation, could now attend Cathedral Preparatory Seminary in Elmhurst. While Monsignor Robert Welsh served as Rector of the two schools together, Father George

Archbishop Bryan J. McEntegart (1957-1968)

❖ *Chapel, Seminary of the Immaculate Conception, Huntington.*

❖ *St. Bernard, Mill Basin (1961)*

V. Fogarty was appointed Vice-Rector for the Queens school, which was designed to hold a capacity of four hundred students.

In September 1967, a separate college seminary was established in Douglaston. Until then seminarians would have spent their two years of college at the Brooklyn school and would finish the last two at the seminary in Huntington. Now college seminarians would study and live at Cathedral College of the Immaculate Conception before moving on to theology. The dedication Mass took place on December 8, 1967. By that time, however, McEntegart was extremely ill,

❖ *Monsignor James F. Coffey (1908-)*

and could not attend. Auxiliary Bishop Charles R. Mulrooney, President of Cathedral College from 1952 to 1959, presided at the Mass in his absence.

In his book *A City with Foundations*, Monsignor Michael J. Cantley aptly chronicles the changing nature of seminary life. Since 1957, the Seminary of the Immaculate Conception at Huntington had served as the major seminary for both Brooklyn and Rockville Centre. Under the Rector, Monsignor James F. Coffey (1963-1973), the seminary implemented the council's decrees as they applied to priestly formation. In the study of theology, there was a movement away from classic theological manuals toward a greater emphasis

Archbishop Bryan J. McEntegart (1957-1968)

❖ *Archbishop McEntegart at the Annual Seminarians Luncheon, January 1967.*

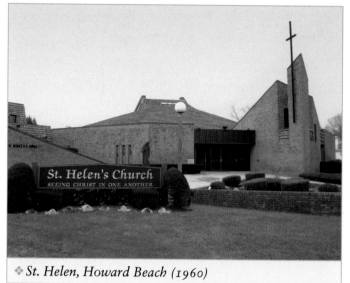

❖ *St. Helen, Howard Beach (1960)*

❖ *A Nursing Sister of the Sick Poor, March 1962.*

McEntegart promoted a close fraternal bond with his priests. One of the means he chose to accomplish that goal was the formation of the Priests Senate. The senate's first meeting took place in December 1966, in the basement of the Chancery Residence. Senate meetings were to be held each month, and three committees were formed: Religious Education, Parish Practices, and a Committee on Race Relations. The Senate gave close attention to urgent pastoral problems facing the Church both nationally and locally.

In the urban metropolis that made up the Diocese of Brooklyn, the particularly pressing issues they identified were race relations, employment and housing. They debated whether a priest coordinator or a vicar should be appointed for inner city ministry. In 1968, the Kerner Commission Report, a federal investigation into civil unrest, concluded that racial unrest in America was worse than ever. The Priests Senate convened a special session to discuss the report, and concurred with its conclusion. New York City was indeed moving toward two societies: one black and one white, separate and unequal. The senate ended its meeting with a call to action, to eradicate the evil of racism.

The Renewal of Religious Life

The renewal of religious life was not a movement that began with Vatican II, but the council undoubtedly gave it greater impetus. In November 1956, the Conference of Major Superiors of Women (now the Leadership Conference of Women Religious) was formed to promote closer bonds between the

on the role of Sacred Scripture and the significance of doctrinal development. In 1965, the initial revision of the Seminary Rule was implemented. In 1966, team teaching of certain courses was introduced into the program. Seminarians were assigned to teach in CCD programs once a week and to visit local hospitals. To meet the changing needs of the times, the study of group dynamics was introduced to the curriculum.

Archbishop Bryan J. McEntegart (1957-1968)

❖ *Sister Charles Veronica, C.S.J., at St. Augustine School, 1960.*

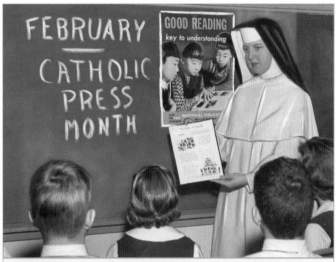

❖ *Sister Marie Andre, O.P., reminds her students that February is Catholic Press Month, 1960.*

❖ *First Mass at Our Lady of Hope, Middle Village, July 1960.*

❖ *Mater Christi High School, 1962.*

various communities and to study new ways of improving the effectiveness of their respective apostolates. In 1962, on the eve of the council, Belgian Cardinal Leon-Joseph Suenens' book *The Nun in the Modern World* challenged religious to reexamine their apostolic life. Suenens pointed out that all Christians, most especially religious, had an obligation to spread the Gospel by their direct and personal action.

On October 28, 1965, Pope Paul VI proclaimed the Decree on the Adaptation and Renewal of Religious Life, *Perfectae Caritatis*. The decree called for religious to rediscover their founder's charism, urging that

> *the spirit and aims of each founder should be faithfully accepted and retained, as indeed should each institute's sound traditions...*

This process of rediscovery would be undertaken within the changing context of the times and in response to the Church's current needs. In the Diocese of Brooklyn, which had been blessed from the start with numerous religious communities, men and women religious began to reflect on the meaning of the conciliar decree, so they might respond more fully to the pastoral demands of a diocese whose ethnic composition was rapidly changing.

As the communities considered the meaning of communal life, its structures, and its prayer forms, many expanded the scope of their apostolic missions. During the 1960's and into the 1970's, Sister Peggy Linahan, a member of the Sisters of Notre Dame De Namur (S.N.D.), became a pioneer in promoting the Diocese's use of educational television. An increasing

Archbishop Bryan J. McEntegart (1957-1968)

SISTER MARY ANTOINETTE, D.W. (1913-1964)

Born in Manhattan to Italian immigrant parents, Ann Donniacuo grew up in St. Mary's parish, Long Island City. Her parents worked at a local Italian restaurant. As a young girl, she spent a summer in Commack, Long Island, that changed her entire life. There the St. Vincent de Paul Society ran a camp for underprivileged children, which was staffed by the Daughters of Wisdom. This experience influenced her decision to enter the congregation, where she made her profession on February 2, 1939. She took the name Sister Mary Antoinette.

From 1939 to 1951, Sister Mary Antoinette taught at Our Lady of Wisdom Academy in Ozone Park. While she was there she realized her vocation to serve as a missionary, and the hope of being able to offer her life as a martyr. Her missionary life began in 1952 at Nyasaland (now Malawi), where she served for six years. In 1961, she went to the Congo, where she worked with eleven European Daughters of Wisdom and three Congolese nuns on the island of Isangi. There they ran a school, an orphanage, and a hospital. As political conditions worsened, family and friends pleaded with her to return to the United States, but she refused.

In October 1964, Congolese rebels occupied Isangi. On November 19, the woman known as the "American Nun" was attacked, beaten, and murdered. Her body was thrown into the Congo River. Bishop John J. Boardman, who had given her the missionary cross she wore, presided over her funeral Mass at St. Mary Gate of Heaven Church in Ozone Park. In 1967, the Daughters of Wisdom returned to the Congo where they continue to minister to God's people.

percentage of male and female religious became more actively engaged in healthcare ministry, social work, youth work and social justice issues. For many communities, the study of Spanish language and Hispanic/Latino culture became a priority.

Sister Rose Patricia O'Leary, O.P., was one of the many religious women who enrolled in the Spanish Language Institute at Bishop Ford High School during the 1960's. In addition to her pastoral ministry at St. Joseph's parish in Long Island City, every Saturday she took the train to Fort Greene, where she worked with teenage dropouts. In 1964, Sister Barbara Ozelski, R.S.M., went to Panama, where the Brooklyn Sisters of Mercy had established a house in 1959. For nearly four decades, she has ministered to the people of Panama through her teaching and her involvement in social justice.

Since 1851, the Christian Brothers had run schools for boys in Brooklyn. In response to the borough's

Archbishop Bryan J. McEntegart (1957-1968)

❖ *Bishop Loughlin High School students, 1960.*

❖ *St. Francis Preparatory School, 1967.*

❖ *Bishop McEntegart with the Carmelite Sisters at Madonna Residence, 1962.*

❖ *Nuns, priests and brothers took an active part in the Civil Rights Movement.*

changing ethnic composition, they expanded their outreach to the city's newer ethnic and racial groups while maintaining their traditional education apostolate. In 1971, they expanded their apostolate even further as Bishop Loughlin High School became a coeducational institution. In his history of the Franciscan Brothers of Brooklyn, Brother Emmett Corry notes that the 1960's was a period of intense reflection and reevaluation by the Brothers as they too responded to the changing face of Catholic life in Brooklyn and Queens. Before the council, in 1959, as the demand for lay retreats grew, the Passionists, a community of priests and brothers,

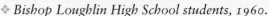

expanded the facilities of Bishop Molloy Retreat House in Jamaica.

During McEntegart's episcopate, new religious communities entered the Diocese. In 1962, the Franciscan Sisters of the Atonement came to St. Jerome's parish in Flatbush at the request of the pastor, Auxiliary Bishop Charles R. Mulrooney. Just before the Sisters arrived, St. Jerome's had conducted a parish census. As a follow-up to the census, the Sisters carried out home visitations throughout the

❖ *Residence of the Apostolic Oblates, Our Lady of Miracles, Canarsie.*

Archbishop Bryan J. McEntegart (1957-1968)

❖ *Cardinal Laurian Rugambwa visits Our Lady of Victory, Bedford-Stuyvesant, 1965.*

❖ *Monsignor Archibald V. McLees, Pastor of St. Pascal Baylon, St. Albans, receives a flag from the local Catholic War Veterans Chapter, 1963.*

parish. The parish visitations became an effective means of interpersonal contact between the people of the parish and the sisters. As a means of evangelization to a parish whose ethnic diversity was increasing throughout the decade, the visitations were an effective pastoral outreach.

In addition to new religious orders, a new form of consecrated life also began to grow in Brooklyn. In 1950, the Secular Institute of the Apostolic Oblates

was founded by Bishop Guglielmo Giaquinta, who had formed the worldwide Pro Sanctity Movement in 1947. Bishop Giaquinta sought to reawaken a vision of the universal call to holiness. In 1965, the Apostolic Oblates, a community of consecrated single lay women offering their lives to God, came to St. Barbara's in Bushwick. Their work included offering retreats, days of prayer, and parish ministry. Since 1975, the Oblates have resided in Canarsie at Our Lady of Miracles parish.

Brooklyn Catholics and the Civil Rights Movement

Throughout the 1960's, Brooklyn Catholics, priests, religious and laity, actively participated in the struggle for civil rights. They attempted to bring healing to the racial unrest in American cities by implementing the gospel virtues of justice, solidarity, and love. In 1965, Bishop McEntegart brought Cardinal Laurian Rugambwa of Tanzania to visit Our Lady of Victory in Bedford-Stuyvesant, a neighborhood that had been torn apart by riots the previous year. The first African Cardinal in the world, Rugambwa's 1965 visit to Brooklyn illustrated the universality of the Church far better than any sermon could do.

In the summer of 1963, religious leaders of all denominations voiced their outrage at the church bombings in Birmingham, Alabama, which resulted in the death of four young girls. That August, the "March on Washington" drew more than 200,000 participants. Among these were thousands of Catholics: clergy, religious, seminarians and laity from throughout the nation. Washington Archbishop Patrick O'Boyle delivered the invocation at this historic gathering.

In the fall of 1963, the Brooklyn Catholic Interracial Council sponsored a day-long conference on racism, which was attended by two hundred people. At the conference, Bishop McEntegart, fresh from his experience at the Vatican Council, reflected on the universality of the Church and called for an end to racial discrimination. At the same time, however, the keynote speaker, Monsignor Francis X. Fitzgibbon, feared a lukewarm response to this problem by local religious leaders. During the fall, Monsignor Archibald V. McLees, Pastor of St. Pascal Baylon in St. Albans,

Archbishop Bryan J. McEntegart (1957-1968)

❖ *Holy Rosary School, Bedford-Stuyvesant, 1966.*

❖ *Angel Guardian Home, ca. 1962.*

❖ *St. Pascal Baylon, St. Albans (1930)*

preached at the annual Red Mass in St. Agnes Cathedral, Rockville Centre. McLees, a leading Catholic advocate of civil rights, labeled racism an unavoidable and fundamentally moral and religious issue. To turn a "cold shoulder" to this issue, he stressed, was sinful.

McLees led a Brooklyn delegation to Rome in October 1963 for the canonization of the Ugandan martyrs. This was the only diocesan delegation from the Western hemisphere. In 1964, the Diocese joined other denominations in sponsoring the Metropolitan New York Conference on Religion and Race. In May 1966, McEntegart directed that every parish announce his pastoral letter condemning housing discrimination. In 1963, he required all contractors working on diocesan projects to integrate their workforce as much as possible.

Catholic Charities

From the start, charity has been a central component of the Catholic experience on Long Island. Outreach to the most needy and vulnerable, to the marginalized and the poor, to the abused and the homeless, to the refugee and the imprisoned, to the immigrant, has been a primary aspect of Catholic charity in Brooklyn, an expression of fidelity to Christ's radical message of love to those most in need, a fulfilling of the historical mission of His Body, the Church. Bishops, priests, religious and laity have all cooperated in accomplishing this mission.

In 1957, Bishop McEntegart came to Brooklyn with a well-deserved reputation as a national leader in Catholic Charities. Over the next eleven years, he oversaw an expansion and redevelopment of its activity in Brooklyn and Queens. After Castro's takeover of Cuba in 1959, as thousands of Cubans fled their native land, McEntegart established the Cuban Refugee Resettlement Center. Working with Catholic Relief Services and Catholic

Archbishop Bryan J. McEntegart (1957-1968)

MONSIGNOR ARCHIBALD V. MCLEES (1905-1995)

Born in Brooklyn in 1905, Archibald McLees studied at St. Francis Preparatory School and Cathedral College. His 1924 Cathedral College yearbook records that when he first visited the school, he looked around and said, "I think I'll stay here." From 1924 to 1930, McLees pursued his priestly studies in Rome. After he was ordained a priest in 1929, he stayed in Rome for another year to complete a doctorate at the University of the Propagation of the Faith. When he returned to Brooklyn in 1930, he was assigned to St. Saviour's parish in Park Slope, where he served until 1938. From 1930 to 1948, he also taught French at Cathedral College. After 18 years of teaching, he returned to parish work as Pastor of Holy Rosary, which was by then a largely African-American parish in Bedford-Stuyvesant.

During his fifteen years at Holy Rosary, Father McLees (in 1961 he was made a Monsignor) became active in the civil rights movement. In 1963, he was appointed Pastor of St. Pascal Baylon. Established in St. Albans in 1930, the parish was undergoing a major demographic shift as the neighborhood's African-American population dramatically increased. He remained there until his formal retirement in 1977.

Monsignor McLees, however, never really "retired." Throughout his 65 years of priesthood, he served on numerous committees in the cause of racial and social justice. For almost forty years, he was Moderator and Director of the Brooklyn Catholic Interracial Council. For three decades, he was a board member of the NAACP Chapters in both Brooklyn and Queens. From 1967 to 1978, he served on the NAACP's national board of directors. At Holy Rosary, Monsignor McLees baptized heavyweight boxing champion Floyd Patterson. In 1965, he marched with Dr. Martin Luther King, Jr., in Selma, Alabama.

McLees also served on the Diocesan Ecumenical Commission and the Catholic-Jewish Ecumenical Committee. On May 15, 1995, Monsignor Robert McCourt delivered the homily at Monsignor McLees' funeral Mass. McCourt, then Pastor of St. Pascal Baylon, described him as a true champion of social justice, a man who balanced brilliance with a deep Christ-like humility,.

Charities in the Archdiocese of Miami, thousands of Cuban refugees were brought to Brooklyn. In Brooklyn, Catholic Charities helped them to find employment and housing, and provided basic legal assistance.

In July 1961, Father Francis J. Mugavero, Director of Charities for Queens County, was named Secretary to the Bishop for

Charities. In September, Father Joseph M. Sullivan, who had just completed a Master's in Social Work from Fordham, was appointed Director of the Child Care Division. While attending Manhattan College, Sullivan had pitched in the minor leagues before he decided

❖ *St. Laurence, East New York (1964)*

Archbishop Bryan J. McEntegart (1957-1968)

❖ *Monsignor Mugavero with Bishop McEntegart, 1963.*

❖ *Bishop McEntegart at St. Joseph Hall, 1961.*

❖ *Father Joseph Sullivan at Catholic Charities, 1964.*

❖ *St. John's Hospital, February 1964.*

to pursue the priesthood. As President Lyndon B. Johnson declared war on poverty, and as Vatican II further articulated the Church's social justice teaching, Sullivan saw that Catholic Charities had to take the lead in the war against poverty.

Under Monsignor Mugavero, Robert Murphy writes, Catholic Charities moved towards decentralization, and "was moving out into the city." Neighborhood outreach had begun in Bedford-Stuyvesant, with anti-

poverty programs such as the St. John the Baptist Community Center and the St. Joseph Head Start Center. The center at St. John's was unique in that it was the only federally funded anti-poverty program run by a single parish. In 1968, the Crown Heights Project established community centers in a growing Caribbean community. In Queens, the Martin De Porres Center sponsored anti-poverty programs as well as recreational programs for teens in Astoria's public housing projects.

Archbishop Bryan J. McEntegart (1957-1968)

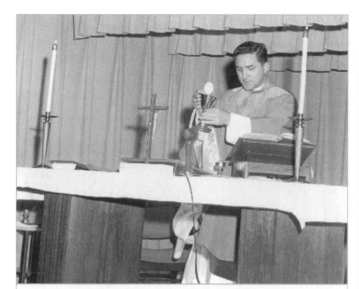

❖ *Father George T. Deas teaching the New Order of the Mass, 1965.*

❖ *St. Joseph's College hosts an exhibit of Byzantine Rite vestments, 1961.*

during the 25th Annual Conference on Eastern Rites, he presided at the Divine Liturgy of St. John Chrysostom.

One of the most important topics of discussion at Vatican II was the role and influence of the Blessed Virgin Mary in Catholic life. In *Lumen Gentium*, the Dogmatic Constitution on the Church (1964), Mary's role was affirmed within the context of Catholic doctrine and devotion. In November 1964, Pope Paul VI proclaimed Mary the "most holy Mother of the Church." While the post-conciliar era saw a decline

in some forms of Marian devotion, the immigrant nature of Brooklyn diocesan life ensured that Mary would continue to be honored within its various ethnic traditions.

Both before and after Vatican II, Marian celebrations were an integral part of community life throughout the Diocese. As previously noted, Hispanic/Latino parishes honored Mary within the context of their particular ethnic traditions. This was true as well of the Diocese's Eastern European Catholics. In 1966, the Diocese celebrated the thousandth anniversary of

❖ *St. Columba, Marine Park (1967)*

Archbishop Bryan J. McEntegart (1957-1968)

❖ *Bishop McEntegart at Our Lady of Lebanon, February 1964.*

❖ *The thousandth anniversary of Christianity in Poland is celebrated at St. Stanislaus Kostka, Greenpoint, 1966.*

Christianity's arrival in Poland. Here Marian devotion focused on Our Lady of Czenstochowa, who occupies a focal point in the faith life of Polish Catholics throughout the world. Public events such as these reflected a deep historical, cultural, theological, sociological, and anthropological understanding of Mary and the Church. They also displayed an understanding of the Church's corporate ecclesial identity in the public square.

For Catholics, an especially important dimension of the beauty of holiness is seen in the public reverence the Church renders to her saints. As models of holiness, the saints represent the completion of the human pilgrimage, whereupon they are enrolled among the "*cloud of witnesses*" (Hebrews 12:1). As such, they bear eternal witness to the Holy One of God, Jesus Christ. In 1963, the beatification of Mother Elizabeth Ann Seton (1774-1821), the New York convert who founded the Sisters of Charity, was followed with great interest by the local media, and was the focus of local ecumenical celebrations. The lives of the martyrs and saints remind us that the call to holiness is given to all. Each of the 16 conciliar documents confirmed that foundational baptismal vocation.

On November 18, 1965, *Apostolicam Actuositatem*, the Decree on the Apostolate of the Laity, was published. The decree, which outlined the theological rationale of the lay apostolate, was not an attempt to clericalize

❖ *For nearly seventy years, Monsignor Mieczyslaw Mrozinski (1888-1984) was associated with Ss. Cyril and Methodius parish in Greenpoint.*

the laity. Rather, it highlighted the complementary roles of priestly ministry and the "distinctive task" of the layperson to renew the temporal order. Before and after Vatican II, the laity's role in the life of the Church was

Archbishop Bryan J. McEntegart (1957-1968)

THE CATHOLIC LAITY

".... the laity are made to share in the priestly, prophetical and
kingly office of Christ; they have therefore, in the Church and
in the world, their own assignment in the mission of the whole
People of God. In concrete, their apostolate is exercised when
they work at the evangelization and sanctification of men; it is
exercised too when they endeavor to have the Gospel spirit
permeate and improve the temporal order, going about it in
a way that bears clear witness to Christ and helps forward
the salvation of men. The characteristic of the lay state being
a life led in the midst of the world and of secular affairs, laymen
are called by God to make of their apostolate, through the vigor
of their Christian spirit, a leaven in the world."
(from the Decree on the Apostolate of The Laity, #2)

❖ *Precious Blood, Coney Island (1927)*

❖ *Lay-Clergy Dialogue, Sacred Heart, Cambria Heights,
April 1967.*

Archbishop Bryan J. McEntegart (1957-1968)

❖ *In 1967, Father George V. Fogarty was appointed first Director of the Pastoral Institute.*

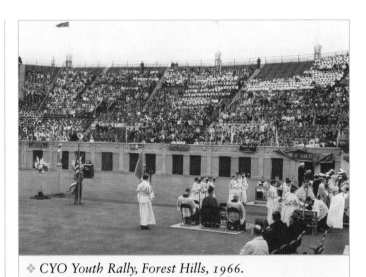

❖ *CYO Youth Rally, Forest Hills, 1966.*

❖ *Monsignor Charles E. Diviney meets with local Pastors at a Lutheran-Catholic Dialogue, April 1968.*

a main concern for Bishop McEntegart. In his speeches and sermons, McEntegart often quoted Pope Pius XII:

> *the laity do not belong to the Church... they are the Church. When you see bishops or priests, do not think of them as persons apart from yourselves. All of us together are the Church.*

In the years following the council, new forms of lay participation emerged: in the form of parish councils and liturgy committees, as well as increased lay participation in various diocesan committees. In their annual conventions, the Diocesan Council of Catholic Women addressed the theology, the spirituality and the apostolate of the Catholic laywoman, in light of the discussions which had taken place at the council. The retreat movement offered laypeople, often through their parish societies, weekends for spiritual enrichment. In March 1967, the Diocesan Priests' Day of Recollection was offered by two lay people; the topic was "What the Layman looks for in a Priest?" In 1967, the Pastoral Institute was established at Cathedral College, which provided ongoing theological formation for laity, religious, and priests, in light of the conciliar experience.

Nowhere was the vitality of Catholic life in Brooklyn and Queens more evident than in the various programs for the youth. Parishes sponsored social outreach programs that reflected council's sensitivity to social justice issues. Through the Diocesan Scouting program, Scouts of all ranks, arrayed in their colorful uniforms, assisted at various functions at both the parochial and diocesan levels. It was during the 1960's that the CYO

underwent a major diocesan-wide expansion. In 1963, at the Forest Hills Tennis Stadium, some 14,000 Catholic youth attended the Twenty-fifth Annual Queens CYO Rally, where Auxiliary Bishop John J. Boardman encouraged them to celebrate their faith.

During the Vatican II era, ecumenical relations took on a new life. In *Unitatis Redintegratio*, the Decree on Ecumenism (November 21, 1964), the council called for the restoration of Christian unity. In *Nostra Aetate*, the Declaration on the Relation of the Church to Non-Christian Religions (October 28, 1965), the council appealed for greater dialogue and collaboration with other religions. At Jerusalem in 1964, Pope Paul VI and the Patriarch Athenagoras I of Constantinople mutually lifted the censures of excommunication which had been imposed in 1054. This event marked an historic development in Catholic-Orthodox relations.

Archbishop Bryan J. McEntegart (1957-1968)

❖ *Our Lady of the Skies, JFK Airport.*

❖ *Father Joseph Konrad speaks at a local synagogue, 1971.*

On the local level, the effort to develop better relations among Catholics, Protestants, and Jews made noticeable progress. In September 1964 at the Flatbush Dutch Reformed Church, Monsignor Charles E. Diviney, Pastor of St. Charles Borromeo Church in Brooklyn Heights, addressed an audience of three hundred Brooklyn ministers on Protestant-Catholic dialogue. Faith communities worked together in the civil rights movement. Operation Yorkville, a project directed by a priest, a rabbi, and a minister sought to keep obscene literature away from children. Out of this group grew the national organization known as Morality in Media. Other joint ventures, such as soup kitchens organized by Jewish and Catholic veteran groups, took place in many neighborhoods.

In 1966, Archbishop McEntegart established the Diocesan Ecumenical Commission. The Chairman of the Commission was Father Joseph Konrad; its members included Fathers Michael J. Cantley and Kenneth Morgan. The Commission was charged with multiple tasks, such as sponsoring interfaith prayer services, promoting greater interaction between the clergy of the different faith denominations, and working together with other faiths on social justice issues.

In 1957, at age 64, at a time when most people are approaching retirement, Bryan J. McEntegart began a new job, the latest stage in an already distinguished life of priestly service. He came to Brooklyn as a nationally renowned educator and child welfare advocate. Under his leadership, Brooklyn Catholics were well prepared to meet the various challenges and changes that faced their neighborhood, their nation, the Church and the

❖ *In 1967, Archbishop McEntegart celebrated his fiftieth anniversary of priesthood at St. James Cathedral. Here he is accompanied by two future Bishops, Monsignors John J. Snyder and Francis J. Mugavero.*

world. A participant in one of the greatest religious events of the twentieth century, Bishop McEntegart worked with the people of the Diocese in allowing the spirit of the Second Vatican Council to permeate Catholic life.

EASTERN RITE PARISHES

Seen here are some of the 11 Eastern Rite parishes in the Brooklyn Diocese serving the needs of Maronites, Melkites, Byzantine Ruthenians, Ukrainians, Armenians and Coptic Catholics.

❖ *Annunciation of the B.V.M. (Ukrainian), Fresh Meadows.*

❖ *St. Mary Protectress (Ukrainian), Ozone Park.*

❖ *Resurrection Coptic Catholic Church, Park Slope.*

❖ *Holy Cross (Ukrainian) Church, Astoria.*

This stained glass window is from Resurrection, Gerritsen Beach (1924).

NEW HEAVEN NEW EARTH

HISTORY OF THE DIOCESE OF BROOKLYN

CHAPTER SIX

"A Time for Hope": Bishop Francis J. Mugavero (1968-1990)

Changes in Church and World

Without doubt, 1968 was the most tumultuous year in a tumultuous decade. In January, a successful offensive by North Vietnamese troops made it clear that an American victory in Southeast Asia was in doubt. In April, Dr. Martin Luther King was assassinated in Memphis, and the ensuing race riots tore the nation apart.

At Columbia University in New York City, student protestors took over the campus for a week. In June, Robert F. Kennedy was assassinated in Los Angeles. Antiwar protestors surrounded the 1968 Democratic convention while casualties in Vietnam escalated. A counterculture that questioned the relevance of authority and traditional moral standards grew among the nation's youth. Throughout the nation, 1968 was a year of confusion and disarray, signaling the breakdown of any kind of consensus in American life.

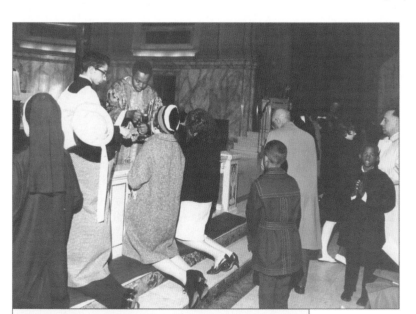

❖ *Memorial Mass for Dr. Martin Luther King, Jr., at St. James Cathedral, April 1968.*

According to Professor Philip Gleason of Notre Dame, 1968 also witnessed the breakdown of consensus in American Catholic life. Catholics divided over a variety of issues: the Vietnam War, racial tension, urban unrest, women's rights and the "sexual revolution." They also began to publicly differ on the nature of ecclesial authority, the meaning of Vatican II, and the very nature of dissent itself. Urban unrest and neighborhood change affected Catholics as schools and parishes closed or reduced their services. A mass exodus from the priesthood and religious life began. A radical drop in vocations signaled, for many, the end of an era.

Bishop Francis J. Mugavero (1968-1990)

❖ *Our Lady of Victory, Bedford-Stuyvesant, 1968.*

❖ *Father John P. McCullagh, a U.S. Army Chaplain, distributes communion in Vietnam, 1967.*

❖ *Visitation of the B. V. M., Red Hook (1854)*

Perhaps the most dramatic controversy surrounded Pope Paul VI's encyclical *Humanae Vitae*, issued on July 25, 1968, which addressed the question of birth control. The availability of the birth control pill had spawned debate over the morality of contraception, and Pope John XXIII established a committee to address the issue. Although the committee recommended modification in the Church's teachings on this subject, Pope Paul VI chose to reaffirm the Church's traditional teaching. In *Humanae Vitae*, he wrote that "each and every marital act must of necessity retain its intrinsic relationship to the procreation of human life." The encyclical, writes the Jesuit historian F. Michael Perko, "marked the beginning of an increasing tendency of American Catholics to pick and choose which Church teachings they would follow."

On September 12, 1968, at Our Lady of Perpetual Help in Bay Ridge, Monsignor Francis J. Mugavero was consecrated and installed as the fifth Bishop of Brooklyn. In his homily, Father George T. Deas, a spiritual director at Cathedral College in Douglaston, captured the spirit of the time: "The winds of change are blowing hard around this world of ours. Change is the most common experience of our lives." Under

Bishop Francis J. Mugavero (1968-1990)

❖ *Most Precious Blood, Astoria (1922)*

❖ *Bishop Mugavero's Installation Mass, September 1968.*

❖ *Home Mass at Our Lady of Mercy, Forest Hills, July 1969.*

❖ *SS. Peter & Paul Youth Center, Williamsburg, 1971.*

Bishop Mugavero, the Diocese would address modern life through the lens of Vatican II, to formulate an authentically Catholic response. An increasingly secular mentality was being reinforced by philosophical subjectivism, moral relativism, and an intense individualism. This outlook led to a weakened respect for human life's dignity.

The Changing Face of Brooklyn and Queens

At the beginning of the twentieth century, the American Catholic Church was a predominantly working class, urban immigrant body. By 1968, it was no longer concentrated exclusively in the cities, nor was it homogeneously immigrant. After World War II, veterans returning from World War II took advantage of the G.I. Bill to pursue degrees in higher education. They moved into professions that their parents could never have dreamed of, and they began new lives in the growing suburbs. For their children, college was a given, whether it be Notre Dame or St. John's, Hofstra or Harvard. The immigrant neighborhoods that their parents and grandparents had inhabited became a thing of lore, of which they were only dimly aware.

Bishop Francis J. Mugavero (1968-1990)

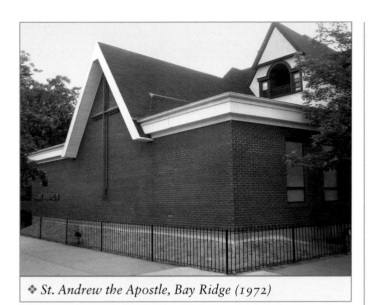

❖ *St. Andrew the Apostle, Bay Ridge (1972)*

❖ *St. Kevin, Flushing (1926)*

The suburbanization process had begun in the 1920's, but was sidetracked by the Depression. A postwar economic boom and the G.I. Bill accelerated the movement as white middle-class families moved out of Brooklyn and Queens to Nassau and Suffolk, which had significant implications for diocesan life. Between 1969 and 1989, Brooklyn and Queens' Catholic population fell from 1.5 to 1.2 million. A 1960's government study found a third of all Brooklyn parishes were in poverty-stricken communities. In 1973, one survey showed that only six percent of the people living in the parish boundaries of Bedford-Stuyvesant's St. Ambrose, formerly a powerhouse of Brooklyn Catholic life, were members of the parish.

During the 1970's, Bishop Mugavero closed nine parishes and 35 schools. At the same time, however, new parishes were formed, such as St. Andrew the Apostle in Bay Ridge and St. Dominic in Bensonhurst, in 1972. The Mugavero years were a time of tremendous innovation as new ministries and outreaches were made in education, in works of charity, in pastoral ministry and in social justice for all the people of Brooklyn and Queens.

In addition to the diocesan archives and the diocesan newspaper, the many changes that have occurred since the Second Vatican Council have been recorded in the *Quinquennial Reports* and in the responses to the *Sesquicentennial Questionnaire.* The

Quinquennial Report is a document drawn up by the various diocesan departments, agencies, and offices in preparation for a diocesan bishop's required, periodic visit to Rome (the "Ad Limina" visit). The visit represents an important time of consultation with the Pope and the Roman dicasteries on matters concerning local Church life: ecclesiastical structures, the activity of Catholic Charity, the mission of Catholic education, various expressions of Catholic spirituality, and relations between the diocesan church and other religious bodies.

Bishop Francis J. Mugavero

Born in Brooklyn on June 8, 1914, Francis John Mugavero was the third of six children born to Sicilian immigrants, Angelo and Rose Pernice Mugavero. The Mugavero family lived above the DeKalb Avenue barbershop that Angelo owned in Bedford-Stuyvesant. In a 1987 interview, Bishop Mugavero recalled that when he told his parents he wanted to be a priest, his father said: "If you're going to be a priest, be a good one." After studying at Cathedral College and at the new seminary in Huntington, he was ordained in 1940.

The young Father Mugavero served as a curate at two Italian parishes, St. Joseph Patron of the Universal Church in Bushwick, and Nativity of the Blessed

❖ *Bishop Mugavero's episcopal coat of arms.*

LOVE ONE ANOTHER

CLOSED PARISHES

Over the years, as neighborhoods changed, some parishes that once served a heavily Catholic community were forced to close. In another sense, however, these parishes live on, in the minds and hearts of their former parishioners. Seen here are a few parishes which may be gone, but are by no means forgotten.

❖ *From 1904 to 1974, St. Lucy served the Italian Catholics of Fort Greene.*

❖ *Founded in 1883, St. Ambrose in Bedford-Stuyvesant was the home parish of Bishop Francis J. Mugavero.*

❖ *St. Alphonsus, founded in 1873, served Greenpoint's German Catholics for over a century.*

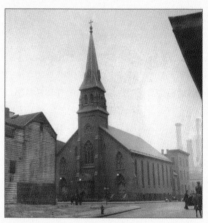

❖ *St. Ann was founded in 1860 to meet the needs of Fort Greene's growing Irish community.*

❖ *St. Monica, Jamaica, as seen in the 1930's.*

❖ *Nativity of Our Blessed Lord, Bedford-Stuyvesant, as seen in the 1920's.*

❖ *In 1853, St. Benedict, Bedford-Stuyvesant, was the first German parish founded by Bishop Loughlin.*

❖ *In 1871, St. Leonard of Port Maurice was founded as a German parish in Bushwick.*

❖ *Located on Hicks Street, St. Peter at one time housed a school, convent, hospital and retreat center.*

Bishop Francis J. Mugavero (1968-1990)

❖ *Bishop Thomas E. Molloy and Father Mugavero with members of the Ferrini League, 1944.*

❖ *Monsignor Mugavero (first row, right) in 1962.*

Virgin Mary in Ozone Park. At night he attended Fordham University's School of Social Service, where one of his professors was Msgr. Bryan J. McEntegart of Catholic Charities in New York. In 1944, Mugavero was assigned to Catholic Charities as assistant director for Queens County. From 1950 to 1961, he served as the director in Queens. At Charities Mugavero was a tireless champion of the poor and needy. Mugavero often remarked that he inherited a strong sense of justice from his family, which he applied to his work at Charities. Bishop Joseph M. Sullivan, who succeeded Mugavero at Charities, said: "He was charity."

Under Bishop McEntegart, Father Mugavero's star began to rise. In 1961, he was appointed the Bishop's Secretary for Charities, and in 1962 he was named a Monsignor. McEntegart relied greatly on Mugavero, in whom he placed great confidence. At the time of his retirement, McEntegart wrote the Apostolic Delegate that Mugavero was the ideal choice for a successor in Brooklyn, one who could shepherd the Diocese through change and turmoil. On July 15, 1968, Monsignor Francis J. Mugavero was appointed the fifth Bishop of Brooklyn. He was the first Brooklynite, and the first Italian-American, to hold that office.

❖ *St. Thomas Aquinas, Flatlands (1885)*

Bishop Francis J. Mugavero (1968-1990)

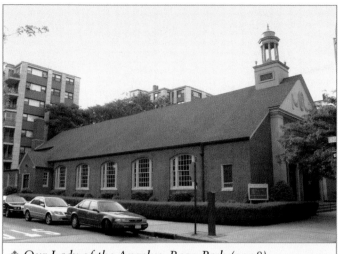

❖ *Our Lady of the Angelus, Rego Park (1938)*

❖ *Parish Procession, Immaculate Conception of the B.V. M., Williamsburg, ca. 1970.*

❖ *Father René A. Valero as Director of the Spanish Apostolate during the 1970's.*

Beginning in 1977, a national rally known as the *Encuentro* raised Hispanic Catholic consciousness. In 1982, the Hispanic Bishops of the United States issued a pastoral letter reminding Hispanics of their religious heritage and calling for a renewal within their community.

In June 1974, the nation's first diocesan congress for Spanish-speaking Catholics was held in Brooklyn. In a meeting described as "tense, but fruitful," committees were established to study the various needs of Brooklyn's Hispanic Catholics: sacramental, educational, social and pastoral. Father John O'Brien, the Diocesan Director of the Spanish Apostolate, was one of many Brooklyn priests who had studied Spanish at Ponce, Puerto Rico. In October 1974, Father René A. Valero was named coordinator for the newly

❖ *St. Rocco, Bush Terminal (1902)*

formed Spanish Apostolate. On November 24, 1980, Valero, along with Monsignor Bevilacqua and Father Joseph M. Sullivan of Catholic Charities, was one of the three new Auxiliary Bishops consecrated at Our Lady of Perpetual Help in Bay Ridge. The new bishops shared their ordinary's concern for charity and immigration.

Bishop Francis J. Mugavero (1968-1990)

❖ *New Auxiliary Bishops, November 1980.*

❖ *Father James Goode, O.F.M., at Our Lady of Charity, Weeksville, September 1973.*

❖ *Lenten procession through Greenpoint, 1979.*

During Mugavero's first ten years as Bishop, the overall population of Brooklyn and Queens decreased by six percent. At the same time, the Hispanic population increased by twenty percent. In 1958, although the Mass was then in Latin, only 12 parishes in Brooklyn and Queens offered homilies in Spanish. By 1979, 99 of the Diocese's 223 parishes offered Mass in Spanish. Back in 1893, St. Barbara was created for German Catholics in Bushwick; in 1901, St. John Cantius was erected as a Polish parish in East New York. By the 1970's, these and many other parishes were ministering to predominantly Hispanic congregations. In sending seminarians and priests to study Spanish, Archbishop McEntegart

had laid an important foundation for the future.

African-American Catholics

As the Diocese's African-American Catholic community grew in size and confidence, Bishop Mugavero established the Council of Black Catholics in 1977. Father James Goode, O.F.M., the Pastor of Our Lady of Charity in Weeksville, served as the Council's first President. A national leader in the black Catholic community, Father Goode brought a charismatic style of leadership to his new role. In 1980, Bishop Mugavero established the Office of Black Ministry. Carole Norris Greene, who had been Public Relations Director for the National Office of Black Catholics in Washington, D.C., was appointed the first Director.

In 1984, the nation's ten African-American Bishops issued a pastoral letter, *What We Have Seen and Heard*, calling on Black Catholics to a new evangelization. A year earlier, Brooklyn's Black ministry office organized the Diocese's first Black Catholic Revival at St. James Cathedral. During the 1980's, the office promoted evangelization through programs highlighting African culture, an annual Black Liturgy workshop and the Mariama Program, which examined the relationship between culture and faith within the context of an Afro-centric religious education.

During the late 1980's, as racial unrest was dividing New Yorkers, Brooklyn Catholic leaders took an

❖ *Bishop Mugavero with the Council of Black Catholics, 1977.*

❖ *Bishop Mugavero meets with local Jewish leaders, 1969.*

active part to promote harmony in the city. In 1988, the Black Ministry office and *The Tablet* sponsored a public forum on racism. Bishop Mugavero issued several public statements on racism, and he issued pastoral letters against racism. At the time of his death, New York Mayor David N. Dinkins called the Bishop "one of our city's greatest racial healers." In 1987, Dinkins' predecessor, Mayor Edward I. Koch, had recognized Mugavero's leadership role in city life when he presented him with the Gold Medal of the City of New York at a reception in Gracie Mansion.

Bishop Mugavero and Ecumenism

Under Archbishop McEntegart, the first significant attempts at Catholic-Jewish relations made headway. In 1966, a Catholic-Jewish Relations Committee was formed in the Diocese, which is believed to be the first of its kind in the United States. Under the leadership of Monsignor Vincent Genova, Pastor of Holy Family in Flatlands, and Rabbi Israel Moskowitz, the committee held its first meeting at the International Hotel in JFK International Airport. Bishop Mugavero continued the work begun under McEntegart, and under his leadership Brooklyn became a national pioneer in Catholic-Jewish relations.

At the 1969 meeting of the National Conference of Catholic Bishops (NCCB), Mugavero was appointed episcopal moderator for the Secretariat

❖ *In 1980, Carole Norris Greene was appointed the first Director of the Black Ministry Office.*

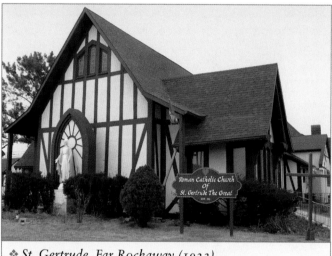

❖ *St. Gertrude, Far Rockaway (1923)*

for Catholic-Jewish Relations, a position he held for nineteen years. In addition to this role, he also served as Chair of the Bishops' Committee for Catholic-Jewish Relations, and as a member of the International Catholic-Jewish Liaison Committee. In 1970, Mugavero convoked a meeting of fifty local Protestant, Jewish and Catholic leaders to discuss ways of implementing *Nostra Aetate*, Vatican II's declaration on the Church's relationship with non-Christian religions.

During Mugavero's episcopate, the Catholic population of Brooklyn and Queens was about 1.6 million, and the Jewish population nearly 1.2 million. The Catholic-Jewish Relations Committee, at both the local and diocesan levels, promoted understanding through lectures, days of prayer, and

Bishop Francis J. Mugavero (1968-1990)

❖ *Bishop Mugavero with Rabbi Gerald I. Weider at Congregation Beth Elohim, Park Slope, January 1987.*

❖ *St. Fortunata, East New York (1934)*

❖ *St. Camillus, Rockaway Beach (1908)*

interfaith projects that addressed local community issues. In 1975, the Brooklyn Diocese, in conjunction with the Archdiocese of New York and the Diocese of Rockville Centre, published a set of guidelines for Catholic-Jewish relations. Although published in the name of all three ordinaries, in reality the guidelines were Bishop Mugavero's brainchild. They eventually became the basis for the Vatican's own guidelines on Catholic-Jewish relations. In 1973, Paul VI appointed Mugavero a Consultor to the Holy See's Secretariat for Promoting Christian Unity, and B'nai B'rith awarded him the Human Relations Award. In 1989, B'nai B'rith again honored him with the Cardinal Bea Interfaith Award.

Under Mugavero, ecumenism, strengthened by the spirit of the council, flourished on all levels. The annual Week of Prayer for Christian Unity, as well as interfaith study days, highlighted efforts to promote religious harmony in the "City of Churches." In September, 1975, an ecumenical prayer

Bishop Francis J. Mugavero (1968-1990)

❖ *Bishop Mugavero hosts the Week of Prayer for Christian Unity at St. James Cathedral, January 1975*

❖ *Bishop-elect Joseph M. Sullivan throws out the first ball at CYO Night, Shea Stadium, September 1980.*

❖ *Groundbreaking ceremony for a new building at St. John's Home, Rockaway Park, October 1969.*

service honored the canonization of St. Elizabeth Ann Seton. Catholic-Protestant workshops addressed issues such as ethnicity and urban crime. Toward the end of the Mugavero era, the Diocese attempted to establish relations with newer religious groups such as the growing Muslim and Hindu communities in Queens.

Catholic Charities

In 1968, Bishop Mugavero appointed Father Joseph M. Sullivan as the Bishop's Secretary for Charities, the position he had held under Archbishop McEntegart. In the summer before attending Manhattan College, Sullivan pitched in the minor leagues. That fall he decided to pursue the priesthood. Ordained in 1956, Sullivan was sent by McEntegart to Fordham in 1959 for a degree in Social Work. In 1961, he began fulltime work at Charities in the Child Care Division. As director of Charities, Sullivan recommended a complete reorganization of Charities from a highly centralized structure to the neighborhoods.

One of Sullivan's most significant changes was in the field of childcare. Ever since the Roman Catholic Orphan Asylum Society was founded in 1829, men

and women religious had administered orphanages where the children lived under close supervision. Father Sullivan wanted to replace this system with programs that keep children in a community setting, such as day-care centers. In 1969, the Dr. Martin Luther King Memorial Day Care Center opened in Bedford-Stuyvesant at St. Joseph's Hall, which the Sisters of Charity founded in 1873 as an orphanage. This was a change that led to complaint and even protest, but Bishop Mugavero supported Father

THE SAINTS COME TO BROOKLYN

Through the process of canonization, the Church publicly recognizes particular men and women for their lives of heroic virtue and holiness. Over the years, the Brooklyn Diocese has been visited by several of them.

ST. ELIZABETH ANN SETON (1774-1821)

❖ Foundress of the Sisters of Charity, Mother Seton was received into the Catholic Church in 1805. As a young woman she and her family spent summers in Brooklyn.

ST. FRANCES X. CABRINI (1850-1917)

❖ Mother Cabrini's Missionary Sisters of the Sacred Heart established a Brooklyn foundation in the 1890's. She was a close friend of Bishop Charles McDonnell.

ST. KATHERINE DREXEL (1858-1955)

❖ Seen here at Little Flower Home , Wading River, in 1930, St. Katherine's Sisters of the Blessed Sacrament staffed the home during its early years.

VENERABLE SOLANUS CASEY, O.F.M. CAP. (1870-1957)

❖ From 1945 to 1946, Father Solanus was the porter at St. Michael's Friary, East New York.

BLESSED TERESA OF CALCUTTA (1910-1997)

❖ Seen here at Our Lady of Victory, Bedford –Stuyvesant, Mother Teresa's Missionaries of Charity currently have two Brooklyn foundations.

DEACON WILLIAM T. JOHNSON (1930-1989)

Born in New York City, William Johnson attended public and parochial schools. After graduating from Cardinal Hayes High School in the Bronx, he studied for several years at St. Joseph's Seminary, Dunwoodie. After discerning that he was not called to the priesthood, Johnson joined the New York City Police Department in 1955. He went on to serve in several important posts, including Assistant Commissioner and Executive Director of the Civilian Complaint Review Board. While a policeman, he earned a law degree.

After retiring from the Police Department, Johnson worked as an attorney. He was a legal representative at the Brooklyn Legal Services Corporation for Brownsville, Brooklyn. In addition he did extensive pro-bono work for the poor. Johnson and his wife Lydia Berrios lived in the St. Albans section of Queens, where they were active in St. Pascal Baylon parish. There he served as a lector and belonged to the Holy Name Society. He was an active member of the St. Albans Civic Association, where he was a strong advocate for youth programs. At the diocesan level, Johnson was active in the Catholic Interracial Council and the Knights of Columbus. Johnson served on *The Tablet*'s advisory committee and Catholic Medical Center's board of directors. He was also President of the Board of Directors for St. Mary's Hospital, Bedford-Stuyvesant. On December 2, 1978, Johnson was ordained to the Permanent Diaconate by Bishop Francis J. Mugavero.

In 1979, when Pope John Paul II celebrated Mass at Yankee Stadium, Deacon Johnson was one of several deacons who assisted the Holy Father. At his funeral Mass, Bishop Mugavero was the main celebrant. Monsignor D. Joseph Finnerty, whose first parochial assignment was to St. Pascal Baylon, preached the homily. Recently Monsignor Finnerty, now Pastor of St. Kevin's in Flushing, reflected on Deacon Johnson's life. Its highlights, he commented, were loyalty to his wife and family, his love for the Mass, and a commitment to social justice. Deacon Johnson, he concluded, was best characterized as "a man of integrity."

leadership roles in this field. For many years Andrew McArdle taught music at Cathedral College. McArdle also directed the choir at his parish, St. Pancras in Glendale. Parish groups such as the St. Pancras Boys Choir were frequently invited to sing at major liturgical celebrations. Brian Zuar, a 1979 graduate of Cathedral College, formed a Diocesan Choir in 1986, which sang at diocesan liturgical celebrations and performed seasonal concerts.

As Vatican II rearticulated the universal call to holiness, lay men and women responded by assuming new

Bishop Francis J. Mugavero (1968-1990)

❖ *Bishop Mugavero at a rally for the Nehemiah Project, August 1985.*

❖ *Home Mass, St. James Cathedral, April 1968.*

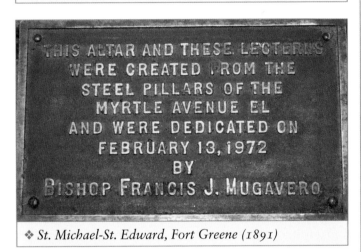

❖ *St. Michael-St. Edward, Fort Greene (1891)*

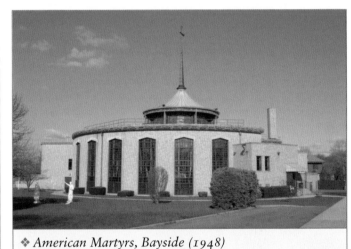

❖ *American Martyrs, Bayside (1948)*

❖ *Andrew McArdle (left, in raincoat) at Good Friday Procession, St. Pancras, Glendale, during the 1970s.*

❖ *Charismatic Rally, Immaculate Conception Monastery, Jamaica, 1977.*

leadership roles in the Church. Some served on parish councils, advisory boards that help pastors in developing the life of the local faith community. Others served as Lay Ministers of the Eucharist, and still others joined priests and deacons at the pulpit as lectors in proclaiming the Word. Throughout Brooklyn

Bishop Francis J. Mugavero (1968-1990)

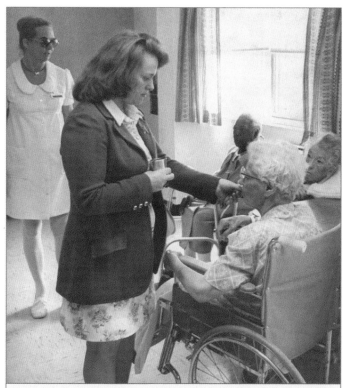

❖ *Eucharistic Minister at Flushing Manor Nursing Home, July 1975.*

❖ *Parish council at work, 1982.*

❖ *Father Joseph Cunningham as Executive Secretary of the Liturgical Commission, ca. 1973*

and Queens, new forms of lay ministry enriched parish life. In responding to the council's call for a rediscovery of scripture, many parishes started Bible study groups. A rediscovery of ancient prayer traditions was evident in the renewed interest in meditative reading and contemplative prayer. Lay people also began to take a leadership role in the retreat movement as directors.

In August 1967, the Christian Family Movement held a conference at the University of Notre Dame.

Out of this conference emerged Marriage Encounter, an organization that challenged married couples to grow spiritually and personally through conferences and weekend retreats. Begun in Spain in 1952, *Encuentro Conyugal* spread from Spain to other Spanish-speaking countries, and then to the United States in its English version. In four decades, the movement has reached a worldwide membership of 1.25 million. The New York area became a center for Marriage Encounter, especially Brooklyn, where many couples are active in the movement. Like the Cursillo, Marriage Encounter is another example of how Hispanic Catholics have influenced the Church in the United States.

The Catholic Charismatic Renewal began during a student retreat at Pittsburgh's Duquesne University in 1966. The movement, which stresses the gift of the Holy Spirit as a road to spiritual renewal, gained a large following during the 1970's through prayer services and healing Masses. In Brooklyn and Queens,

Bishop Francis J. Mugavero (1968-1990)

❖ *A Cursillo at the St. Paul's Center in the early 1970's.*

❖ *St. James Cathedral-Basilica, as depicted by a local artist.*

❖ *St. James Cathedral celebrates its 150th Anniversary, November 1972.*

the movement gained a notable following as Charismatic prayer groups were organized in parishes. Bishop Molloy Retreat House in Jamaica sponsored Charismatic conferences and retreats. In 1983, Bishop Mugavero appointed Monsignor John J. Kean, Pastor Emeritus of St. Peter Claver parish in Bedford-Stuyvesant, as his liaison to the Charismatic Renewal movement.

Two Cathedrals in Brooklyn

In 1972, St. James Cathedral celebrated the 150th anniversary of its founding as Long Island's first Catholic Church. Six years later, St. James marked its 125th anniversary as the diocesan seat. Over the years the neighborhood surrounding the Cathedral, downtown Brooklyn, had become less residential. What was once a thriving neighborhood had become a business district which more often than not emptied out after the workday. In June 1973, St. James parochial school, the first in Brooklyn, closed after 150 years.

In 1977, a Team Ministry organized by Father James Hinchey developed an outreach to disaffected Catholics while seeking to enhance the Cathedral's role as the center of diocesan life. St. James sponsored a series of lectures that received national attention. In two of its programs, "The Shepherds Speak" and

Bishop Francis J. Mugavero (1968-1990)

❖ *Incarnation, Queens Village (1927)*

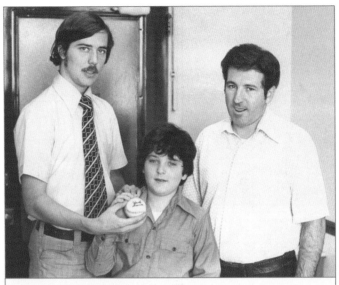

❖ Tablet *sports Writer Ed Wilkinson, 1973.*

"Women as Prophetic Witnesses," bishops and women leaders addressed audiences at St. James on the major ecclesial issues of the day. In addition, the team ministry promoted the arts and various forms of prayer and meditation at the Cathedral.

In 1977, Brooklyn became home to a second Catholic Cathedral: Our Lady of Lebanon in Brooklyn Heights, which became the spiritual home for all Maronite Catholics in the United States. There are now approximately 27,000 Maronite Catholics throughout the United States. Since 1962, the Eparchy's see was in Detroit, but in June 1977 it was transferred to Brooklyn, and its name was changed to the Eparchy of Saint Maron of Brooklyn The choice to relocate was based on the recognition of New York's growing Maronite presence, the "maingate to the United States."

The Tablet

In the year 1968, Patrick F. Scanlan, the "Dean of the American Catholic Press," was 73, and he had been managing editor of *The Tablet* for over fifty years. On June 14, he wrote his last editorial. Don Zirkel, who had been a writer at *The Tablet* for over two decades, was appointed his successor. In June 1968, as he took charge of the paper, Zirkel wrote to Scanlan: "There have been many changes

in the Church since Vatican II, and our job is to present them in the proper perspective." On May 16, 1971, the *New York Times* carried an article entitled "*The Tablet*, Catholic Weekly, Reflects Change." The article stated that under Don Zirkel, the paper's editorial policy had done an "about face":

Once an archconservative defender of the faith, a bitter enemy of liberalism in all its forms and a pioneer 'America Firster,' the newspaper now has not only espoused conscientious objection to the war in Vietnam but also has given frequent support to reform and renewal within the Church.

Nevertheless, Zirkel reminded the *Times* interviewer that the paper's goal was still the same, "to be faithful to the church as the church saw itself, and so there is a sense in which we did not change." Since Vatican II, he said, the Church had "become an open structure, and no longer the monolithic structure it was." While many greeted the new approach favorably, there were many within the Church who did not favor the changes in the paper's editorial policy. Bishop Mugavero, however, gave Zirkel his full support throughout the seventeen years of his editorship. In 1985, he was succeeded by the present editor, Ed Wilkinson, a

❖ *Don Zirkel, Editor of the* The Tablet *(1968-1985).*

173

Bishop Francis J. Mugavero (1968-1990)

❖ *St. Ephrem School, Dyker Heights, 1968.*

❖ *Inner City High School Principals Meeting, 1968.*

Cathedral College graduate who began as a sports writer for the paper in 1970.

Sensitive to the needs of the times, *The Tablet* responded to the Diocese's growing Hispanic population. In June 1972, a monthly Spanish Supplement was added to the paper. On October 5, 1981, the first issue of a Spanish paper, *Nuevo Amanecer* (*New Dawn*), was published. From 1981 to 1994, the paper covered Hispanic news both in Brooklyn and the larger metropolitan region. In 1972, Don Zirkel began an annual separate women's issue, "Ms. Tablet." At the same time, throughout the year, writers (both male and female) were given the opportunity to address issues such as increased leadership roles for women in ecclesial life, the question of women's ordination, and to offer a feminist critique of Catholic theology.

Catholic Education

1964 officially marked the end of the "Baby Boom." Over the next ten years, grammar school enrollment throughout the country declined by 35 percent. In some dioceses, school enrollment dropped nearly twenty percent in a single year. From 1966 to 1968, 637 parochial schools closed in the

❖ *Left : The first issue of* Nuevo Amanecer *appeared in October 1981.*
❖ *Right : Ms. Tablet, 1972.*

United States. Besides the declining birthrate, other factors at work included urban change, a shift in teaching personnel, and a fiscal crisis in the early 1970's. In 1950, fewer than twenty percent of parochial school teachers were lay. By 1979, over seventy percent were. The need to pay lay teachers higher wages than religious, Father F. Michael Perko writes, "transformed the economics of parochial education." Because the school and the parish were so closely interconnected, school closings dramatically transformed the nature of parish life.

In some degree or other, all of these factors were at work in the Brooklyn Diocese, where the Catholic school population would drop by over fifty percent over a twenty-year period. At the start of Bishop Mugavero's episcopate, there were 176,000 children in the parochial school system, and nearly 40,000 in the high schools. In 1990, there were 62,000 in the parochial schools and 20,000 in the high schools. During these years, Mugavero was forced to close forty parochial schools and 14 high schools. As neighborhoods changed, and the majority of the newcomers were not Catholic, parish income decreased to the point where maintaining a school was no longer economically feasible. In many schools, the student body was barely a tenth of what it had been fifteen to twenty years earlier.

In 1970, a diocesan school study concluded that a crisis

GOOD SPORTS

Over the years, the CYO has played a central part in parish life throughout Brooklyn and Queens. Seen here are some photos from *The Tablet*'s sports files taken during the Mugavero years.

❖ *Ascension, Elmhurst.*

❖ *St. Agatha vs. Holy Innocents.*

❖ *Holy Rosary, Bedford-Stuyvesant.*

❖ *Our Lady Queen of Martyrs, Forest Hills.*

❖ *St. Leo, Corona.*

❖ *St. Thomas Aquinas, Flatlands, 1973. Holding the trophy in the front row is future NBA star Chris Mullin.*

Bishop Francis J. Mugavero (1968-1990)

❖ *St. Sylvester, City Line (1929)*

❖ *Bishop Loughlin vs. Holy Cross, March 1976.*

existed in the Catholic school system. Because of declining personnel and increased costs, several religious orders found it difficult to continue their education apostolate in Brooklyn. In June 1972, three communities closed their high schools: the Marianists at Most Holy Trinity in Williamsburg, the Vincentians at St. John's Preparatory School in Bedford-Stuyvesant, and the Jesuits at Brooklyn Preparatory School in Crown Heights. In 1973, Bishop Mugavero and his Superintendent of Schools, Father Franklin E. Fitzpatrick, made the painful decision to close schools whose existence was no longer economically feasible. That year school closings took place in Bedford-Stuyvesant at St. Ambrose, Nativity, St. Benedict, Our Lady of Victory and St. Peter Claver; in Bushwick at Our Lady of Good Counsel and St. Barbara; in Williamsburg at Annunciation and Epiphany. Other schools included St. Joseph in Prospect Heights, St. Matthew in Crown Heights, St. Patrick in Fort Greene, and St. Monica in Jamaica. All Saints High School, founded in 1916, and Bishop McDonnell Memorial School, founded in 1926, also closed their doors.

As Charles Morris notes, however, the school closings were by no means an "abandonment of the inner city." In a 1973 pastoral letter, Bishop Mugavero requested that parishes cluster their resources so as to continue providing a quality Catholic education within their neighborhoods. In response, cluster coordinating councils consolidated elementary schools that had been hit hardest by school closings. As a result, the existing schools were in a much stronger position, capable of offering a greater range of services. In Crown Heights, Unity Catholic School and Holy Spirit School ensured that local children could still receive a Catholic education, while Our Saviour School did the same in Williamsburg.

In many cases, the closed school buildings have continued to serve the needs of the local Church. Catholic Charities has used some of them for housing, such as the former St. Joseph School in Prospect Heights and St. Patrick School in Fort Greene. Bishop McDonnell High School became St. Francis De Sales School for the Deaf. St. Malachy School in East New York closed in 1979, but the former school building now houses the St. Malachy Child Development Center and St. Malachy Head Start. These programs,

Bishop Thomas V. Daily (1990-2003)

❖ *Jornadistas march on Good Friday, Ozone Park, 1997.*

❖ *Mariachi Band at Sacred Heart, Fort Greene, 1996.*

❖ *The Feast of Our Lady of Guadalupe is celebrated at Guardian Angel, Brighton Beach, 1997.*

❖ *In 1991, Father John F. Brogan was named first Director of the Hispanic Ministry Office.*

Hispanic/Latino Catholics

Of all the recent immigrant groups, the Hispanics are the largest. During the last thirty years, the nation's Hispanic population has increased nearly fourfold, from 9.5 million to 35 million. Recent surveys estimate that one out of every eight Americans is of Hispanic descent. Because Catholicism has held a central place in Hispanic culture over the centuries, these demographics have long-term implications for the American Church. In 1999, a report by the Bishops' Committee on Hispanic Affairs, *Hispanic Ministry at the Turn of the New Millenium*, noted that Hispanics then constituted nearly 38 percent of all American Catholics.

Since 1980, New York City's Hispanic population has increased by sixty percent, making it the city's largest minority group. At the same time, a process

❖ *Born in Havana, Monsignor Otto L. Garcia has been Vicar General of the Diocese since 1995.*

Bishop Thomas V. Daily (1990-2003)

❖ *Members of the Diocese's Ghanaian Apostolate.*

❖ *Brooklyn Catholics visit Our Mother of Africa Chapel at the National Shrine in Washington, D.C., 1997*

of diversification has taken place in that community. The increased use of the term Latino is a reflection of this change. Older Hispanic groups such as the Puerto Ricans and Cubans have experienced a slight decline, while newer groups have increased significantly. Between 1980 and 2000, the city's Mexican population grew from 22,000 to 186,000. Similarly, the Colombian and Ecuadorian population respectively increased by 133 percent and 241 percent.

During the first six years of Bishop Daily's episcopate, the Diocese's Hispanic population increased by twelve percent; it has been estimated that some fifty percent of all Catholics in Brooklyn and Queens are Hispanic. Brooklyn has the seventh largest Hispanic population of any American diocese. In 1991, Bishop Daily separated the Spanish Apostolate from the Migration Office to create a separate Hispanic Ministry office. He appointed Father John Brogan, who had many years of experience ministering to

the Hispanic community, as the first director. In Brooklyn and Queens, 113 parishes offer services in Spanish to a diverse and growing Hispanic population.

Catholics of African Descent

Under a series of capable directors, the Office of Black Ministry sought new ways to promote and enhance African-American Catholic life. The Kujenga Retreat ("Kujenga" is the Swahili word for "leadership") for Black teenagers and their families helped promote the "New Evangelization" through its leadership training programs. Throughout the 1990's, the office worked closely with the Racial Harmony Commission to address racism in Brooklyn and Queens. In May 1998, Director Madeline Anderson organized the Diocese's first Black Catholic pilgrimage to the National Shrine of the Immaculate

Bishop Thomas V. Daily (1990-2003)

❖ *Bishop Daily with the Office of Black Ministry staff, 1994*

❖ *The Feast of Corpus Christi is celebrated at St. Jerome, Flatbush, 2000.*

❖ *This statue of Our Lady of Guadalupe stands outside St. Patrick, Long Island City, a parish founded for Irish immigrants in 1868.*

Conception in Washington, D.C. The main object of their visit was the Chapel of Our Mother of Africa, which had been dedicated in August 1997.

During Bishop Daily's episcopate, the number of Catholics of African descent expanded significantly. Included in this group are Haitians, West Indians, and Africans. Brooklyn is currently the largest Haitian city outside of Port-au-Prince. During these years, the Catholic Migration Office created new apostolates for the West Indian, Ghanaian, and Nigerian communities. An increased number of African priests now minister in many Brooklyn and Queens parishes. Like the priests who came to Brooklyn from Europe during the nineteenth century, many of them came here to minister to their people in a strange new world.

The Changing Face of Parish Life

The word "Catholic" means "universal," and nowhere is the Church's Catholicity more evident than it is in the Brooklyn Diocese. Parishes that were started for one particular ethnic group are now home to another, if not several. St. Patrick was founded in Long Island City for Irish immigrants in 1868. Today, a statue of Our Lady Guadalupe stands outside a heavily Mexican parish. In recent years, St. Aloysius in Ridgewood, which began as a German parish, has ministered to a largely Vietnamese community. Recently it has introduced a Sunday Mass in Polish. At nearby St. Matthias, a sign advertises Masses in four languages: English, Spanish, Polish, and German. St. Sebastian's in Woodside is home to a variety of

Bishop Thomas V. Daily (1990-2003)

❖ *Syro-Malabar Rite Catholics at Our Lady of the Snows, North Floral Park.*

❖ *Children celebrate the hundredth anniversary of St. Stanislaus Kostka, Greenpoint (1996).*

❖ *Syro-Malankar Rite Catholics celebrate Mass at the Immaculate Conception Center, Douglaston.*

Latino Catholics, Filipinos and recent Irish immigrants. In Greenpoint, St. Stanislaus Kostka continues to welcome Polish immigrants as it has done since 1896. Of the 14 Masses celebrated each weekend, 12 are in Polish. Parish life in the Brooklyn Diocese, therefore, is a true exercise in multiculturalism.

Eastern Rite Catholics

In another sign of genuine Catholicity, Eastern Rite Catholics continue to find a welcome in the Diocese. From the early 1990's through 2003, Indian Catholics of the ancient Syro-Malabar Rite worshipped at Our Lady of the Snows in North Floral Park. Indian Catholics of the Syro-Malankar Rite worship at the St. Basil Malankara Catholic Mission, which uses the facilities of the Immaculate Conception Center. By the time of the ses-

quicentennial there were 11 Eastern Rite Churches in Brooklyn and Queens.

New Bishops

In August 1994, Bishop Daily ordained two new auxiliary bishops: Monsignor Ignatius A. Catanello, principal of Cathedral Preparatory Seminary, and Father Gerald M. Barbarito, the Diocesan Vice-Chancellor. A graduate of St. Francis College, Bishop Catanello had been a parish priest, Episcopal Vicar, and a Theology professor at St. John's University. He has taken a leading role in Catholic-Muslim relations. Ordained in 1976, Bishop Barbarito served at St. Helen's, Howard Beach, before he was assigned to the Chancery in 1981. In 1999, he was named Bishop of Ogdensburg. On August 28, 2003, he was installed as the fifth Bishop of Palm Beach. In 1997, Monsignor Vincent D. Breen, the Vicar for Education, was appointed Bishop of Metuchen.

Bishop Thomas V. Daily (1990-2003)

❖ *Bishop Daily with Auxiliary Bishops Ignatius A. Catanello and Gerald M. Barbarito, 1994.*

❖ *Brooklyn Catholics proclaim the Gospel of Life during Pope John Paul II's 1995 visit to the Diocese.*

The Teaching Role of the Bishop

In his 1995 encyclical *Evangelium Vitae*, Pope John Paul II noted that there existed in the modern world a growing "culture of death." As the Holy Father called on Catholics to promote a culture of life, Bishop Daily used every means in his power toward this end. Under his leadership, the education office issued guidelines for teaching human sexuality from a Catholic perspective. In 1998, he initiated a series of academic conferences on human life issues. Bishop Daily has long been recognized as a defender of the dignity of human life at every stage.

❖ *A native of Lebanon, Bishop Hector Youssef Doueihi has been Bishop of the Eparchy of St. Maron of Brooklyn since 1996.*

❖ *In 1997, Monsignor Vincent D. Breen (1937-2003), Vicar for Education, was named Bishop of Metuchen.*

Bishop Thomas V. Daily (1990-2003)

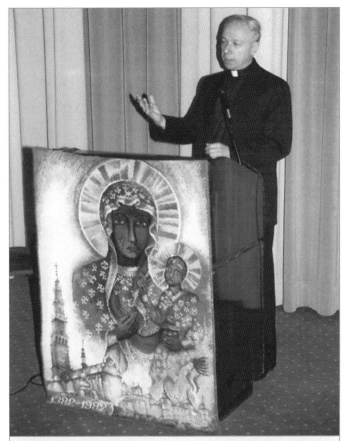

❖ *Since 2001, Monsignor John Strynkowski has been Executive Director of the Secretariat for Doctrine and Pastoral Practice for the Bishops' Conference in Washington, D.C.*

❖ *Bishop Daily prays with the Helpers of God's Precious Infants in Forest Hills.*

❖ *In 1999, Catherine Bala was appointed Director of the Family Life/Respect Life Office.*

Bishop Daily was the first bishop in the United States to lead a prayer vigil with the Helpers of God's Precious Infants. Every month throughout his episcopate, he prayed the rosary before abortion clinics throughout Brooklyn and Queens. Under Evelyn Aquila and her successor Catherine Bala, the Diocesan Office of Family Life/Respect Life has instituted programs that foster an appreciation for every stage of life. Its programs affirm the dignity of the married state, the right to life, and the care for the elderly.

Bishop Daily and the Devotional Life of the Church

Bishop Daily's episcopate witnessed a local resurgence of devotional life, which Pope John Paul II has encouraged as a manifestation of the Church's vitality. Throughout his episcopate, Bishop Daily encouraged eucharistic devotion as the key to the renewal of Catholic life. In 1992 and in 2003, he issued pastoral letters on the Eucharist that stressed both the personal and communal dimensions of eucharistic adoration. In September 1995, the first Diocesan Eucharistic Congress was held at St. John's University, drawing an audience of nearly 10,000. Bishop Daily designated certain parishes throughout the Diocese as centers of Eucharistic adoration. In June 1999, eight Rockaway parishes sponsored a local Eucharistic Congress that drew over one thousand people.

In what is arguably the world's most culturally diverse diocese, Marian devotion not only continued to thrive, but assumed a multiplicity of expressions. Our Lady of Czenstochowa holds a central place in the lives of

Bishop Thomas V. Daily (1990-2003)

❖ *In 1995, a Diocesan Eucharistic Congress was held at the Queens campus of St. John's University.*

❖ *This Memorial to the Unborn at Immaculate Conception, Long Island City, is one of many erected throughout the Diocese since 1973.*

❖ *Cuban Catholics celebrate La Fiesta de Nuestra Señora de la Caridad de Cobre at St. Michael's, Flushing, 1995.*

❖ *Monsignor David Cassato at the Feast of Our Lady of Mount Carmel, Williamsburg, July 1996.*

❖ *Bishop Valero celebrates La Fiesta de Nuestra Señora de Providencia at St. Brigid's, Wyckoff Heights, 1997.*

Our Patroness

The Blessed Virgin Mary, under the title of the Immaculate Conception, is the Patroness of the Diocese of Brooklyn. Nearly one third of our parishes have been named in her honor. Seen here are a few of the ways Our Lady has been depicted throughout the Diocese.

❖ *Our Lady of the Rosary of Pompeii, Williamsburg.*

❖ *St. Catherine of Alexandria, Borough Park.*

❖ *St. Sebastian, Woodside.*

❖ *Incarnation, Queens Village.*

❖ *Resurrection Coptic Catholic Church, Park Slope.*

❖ *Holy Rosary, Bedford-Stuyvesant.*

❖ *Our Lady Help of Christians, Midwood.*

❖ *Our Lady of Fatima, Jackson heights.*

❖ *Mary's Nativity, Flushing.*

❖ *St. Lucy - St. Patrick, Fort Greene.*

❖ *SS. Joachim and Anne, Queens Village.*

❖ St. Bartholomew, Elmhurst.

❖ Our Lady of the Presentation, Brownsville.

❖ Our Lady of the Miraculous Medal, Ridgewood.

❖ St. Anthony - St. Alphonsus, Greenpoint.

❖ St. Boniface, Brooklyn.

❖ St. Pius X, Rosedale.

❖ Our Lady of Consolation, Williamsburg.

❖ Nativity of the B.V.M., Ozone Park.

❖ St. Benedict Joseph Labre, Richmond Hill.

❖ St. Mary Star of the Sea, Carroll Gardens.

❖ Most Precious Blood, Coney Island.

❖ Transfiguration, Williamsburg.

❖ Holy Spirit, Borough Park.

Bishop Thomas V. Daily (1990-2003)

❖ *The relics of St. Therese of Lisieux are brought to St. James Cathedral-Basilica, 1999.*

❖ *Monsignor Octavio Cisneros (on the left) has actively promoted Father Felix Varela's cause for sainthood.*

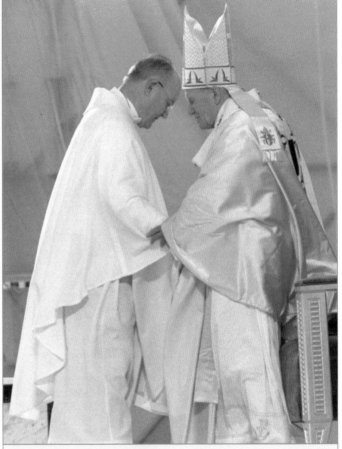

❖ *Pope John Paul II with Bishop Daily at Aqueduct Race Track, October 1995.*

the Diocese's Polish Catholics, while Our Lady of Perpetual Help does the same for Haitian Catholics. Every July in Williamsburg, for nearly a century, Italian Catholics have gathered to honor Our Lady of Mount Carmel. In the Latino community, Mary is venerated under a wealth of titles. Puerto Ricans have a strong devotion to *Nuestra Señora de la Providencia*, Cubans to *Nuestra Señora de la Caridad del Cobre*, Mexicans to Our Lady of Guadalupe, and Dominicans to *Nuestra Señora de Altagracia*. During the Jubilee Year 2000, nearly ten thousand Brooklyn Catholics from all backgrounds came together to join the "Rosary in the Park."

In the Letter to the Hebrews, the saints are described as a great "cloud of witnesses," whose examples encourage us to "persevere in running the race that lies before us, while keeping our eyes fixed on Jesus" (12:1-2). Throughout the Diocese, Haitian Catholics rejoiced in 1996 when Pope John Paul II declared Pierre Toussaint (1786-1853) Venerable. In the fall of 1999, thousands gathered to venerate the relics of St. Therese of Lisieux when they were brought to the Brooklyn Diocese. In April 2001, Hispanic Catholics cheered as Pope John Paul II beatified a layman, Carlos Manuel Rodriguez (1918-1963), the first native of Puerto Rico to be so honored. In 2002, local celebrations commemorated the canonization of Padre Pio. Monsignor Octavio Cisneros, Rector of the Cathedral Seminary Residence, is Vice-Postulator for the canonization cause of Father Felix Varela (1788-1853), a Cuban priest who worked among New York's Irish immigrants in the pre-diocesan era and visited Brooklyn in his capacity as Vicar General of the Archdiocese.

Pope John Paul II Returns to Brooklyn

In the fall of 1995, Pope John Paul II made his fourth visit to the United States. On October 6, he made his second visit to the Brooklyn Diocese, when he celebrated Mass at Aqueduct Race Track in Ozone Park. Over 100,000 people attended the Mass, and nearly seven hundred priests and deacons participated. In his homily, the Pope said, "The Church constantly invokes the Holy Spirit upon individual communities, and today we renew that invocation here, at the Aqueduct Race Track in Queens." He then asked the audience: "In the midst of the magnificent scientific and technological civilization of which America is proud, and especially here in Queens, in New York, is there room for the mystery of God?" For Brooklyn Catholics, the Holy Father's visit was a time of joy and hope.

1996: A Year of Hope

The year 1996 proved to be an eventful one in Diocesan life. In January, Bishop Daily officially launched the "Alive in Hope" campaign. Under the leadership of Monsignor John J. Bracken, the campaign sought to raise fifty million dollars for an endowment that would "prepare the Church of Brooklyn and Queens for the next century." The campaign succeeded far beyond the expectations of many. Like the 1960 Diocesan campaign, Alive in Hope not only reached its goal, but surpassed it by an extraordinary amount. By 1997, $83 million had been pledged. Alive in Hope became a nationwide model for diocesan fundraising campaigns.

From September through December, the Seventh Diocesan Synod (the first since 1926) was held at the Immaculate Conception Center. Approximately five hundred clergy, religious and laypeople participated. During two years of intense preparation, under the direction of Father Michael J. Hardiman, working documents were drafted for the synod which addressed issues of major concern for diocesan life. The topics addressed during the synod included sacraments and liturgy, the priesthood, evangelization and parish life, catechesis and education, pastoral planning and administration, and social issues. Dr. Frank Appah, a native of Ghana and member of St. Matthew's parish

❖ *The Alive in Hope Campaign is advertised at Our Lady of Perpetual Help, Bay Ridge, 1996.*

❖ *Father Frank Caggiano speaks at the Diocesan Synod, 1996.*

in Crown Heights, designed the synod's official logo. Following the working sessions, a redaction committee formulated the participants' concerns in a report submitted to Bishop Daily.

On Pentecost Sunday, 1997, *The Tablet* published the full text of Bishop Daily's response to the Synod

Bishop Thomas V. Daily (1990-2003)

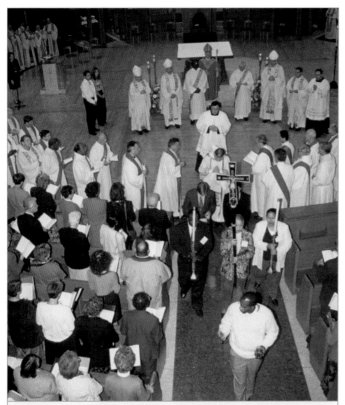

❖ The opening Mass of the Diocesan Synod, 1996.

❖ St. Ignatius, Crown Heights (1908)

❖ Queen of Peace, Kew Gardens Hills (1939)

❖ St. John's Bread & Life Soup Kitchen, Bedford-Stuyvesant.

Report. Stressing the Diocese's cultural and ethnic diversity as a "blessing," he called for Brooklyn Catholics to foster a spirit of collaboration so their respective gifts and talents might be discerned and utilized for the good of the local Church. He also encouraged diocesan agencies to collaborate with parishes in a spirit of common mission. In his 1999 Pastoral Letter, "Synod Implementation," Bishop Daily called for a greater spirit of collaboration within the context of an ecclesial vision of communion. This ecclesial vision of communion provides the context for the mission of the Chancery Office, whose priests, religious women and lay staff exercise a hidden ministry of ecclesial love for the local church. Monsignor Otto L. Garcia, who has worked in the Chancery Office since 1978, serves as both Vicar General and Moderator of the Diocesan Curia. Bishop Daily appointed him Chairman of the Diocesan Sesquicentennial Celebration Committee.

Parish Clusters

As diocesan ordinary, Bishop Daily aimed to inspire Brooklyn Catholics with his vision of communion, collaboration and communication. One of the key means of promoting that vision was through the parish clusters, a regional grouping of parishes throughout the Diocese. The goal of the parish cluster, according to Bishop Daily, is to strengthen the local Church so as

Bishop Thomas V. Daily (1990-2003)

❖ *This carving marking the Jubilee Year is from Holy Trinity, Whitestone.*

❖ *Diocesan Eucharistic Rally at Arthur Ashe Stadium, Flushing, June 2000.*

to more effectively share the "gifts, talents and resources" of the faithful. In September 1999, Daily established the Office of Cluster Planning and Collaboration under Monsignor Cornelius Mahoney, then a Spiritual Director at the seminary in Huntington. Under Monsignor Mahoney, the Cluster Office operates as a resource center and guide for the cluster process. It also publishes a newsletter to promote and enhance communication, while serving as a liaison both with other diocesan agencies and the Bishop.

The Jubilee Year

As the year 2000 approached, Pope John Paul II called upon the Church to undertake a "new evangelization." He therefore proclaimed 2000 as a Jubilee Year of special grace to usher in the third millennium of Christianity. In Brooklyn, Bishop Daily appointed a Commission on Evangelization to prepare

for the Jubilee Year, and he named Father John Costello to direct the Jubilee Office. In 1998, the Diocese implemented "Disciples in Mission," an evangelization program created by the Paulist Fathers' National Catholic Evangelization Association. Disciples in Mission made a special effort to reach out to disaffected and alienated Catholics, while it promoted parish-level evangelization efforts. During 2000, celebrations were held throughout the Diocese at the vicariate, cluster, and parish levels. Reflecting on the significance of the Great Jubilee Year, Bishop Daily wrote:

Everywhere I travel in this Diocese people from almost every land on earth welcome me to their parish…In the Catholic Church there are no strangers, no borders or laws of immigration, no documents or conditions necessary before anyone may enter. The arms of Christ the Savior are opened wide to embrace all who turn to Him.

HISTORY OF THE DIOCESE OF BROOKLYN

Bishop Thomas V. Daily (1990-2003)

❖ *Bishop Daily at Arthur Ashe Stadium, 2000.*

❖ *St. Francis of Paola, Greenpoint (1918)*

The highlight of the Jubilee Year was a Diocesan Eucharistic Rally held in Queens, at Arthur Ashe Stadium, on June 24. Nearly 8,000 people attended the rally, which was highlighted by dance and song representing the various ethnic backgrounds of Brooklyn Catholics. At reconciliation services, nearly eighty priests heard confession in more than a dozen languages. The altar used for the closing Mass was assembled by the Diocesan Theater Guild, and the pieces of the altar were in the shape of brown blocks that were intended to represent the famous brownstones of Brooklyn. The day was a true reflection of the Church's universality, as it is daily lived out in the Brooklyn Diocese.

❖ *Fire Department Chaplain Father John Delendick (center) at Ground Zero.*

September 11, 2001

Without doubt, the single major event of the year 2001 was the terrorist attack on the World Trade Center. On the morning of September 11, two hijacked planes were flown into the Twin Towers. Nearly 3,000 people were lost in an unspeakable and incomprehensible tragedy. No words could capture adequately the pain of the suffering, or the hatred that motivated the attack. Yet from this tragic event, people from all walks of life revealed the meaning of authentic heroism and the power of grace.

Father Mychal Judge, O.F.M., a Chaplain to the New York Fire Department, was the first officially recorded fatality following the attack on the World Trade Center. Born in Brooklyn, Robert Emmett Judge grew up in St. Paul's parish in Cobble Hill. After joining the Franciscans in 1949, he took the name Mychal. A beloved and compassionate priest, he was mourned throughout the city and nation.

In the middle of the debris and smoke, rescue workers noticed that two falling beams had been somehow welded together in the shape of a cross standing about six feet high. Father Brian Jordan, another Franciscan with Brooklyn roots, was there

❖ *This 9/11 Cross stands outside Mary Queen of Heaven, East Flatbush.*

Bishop Thomas V. Daily (1990-2003)

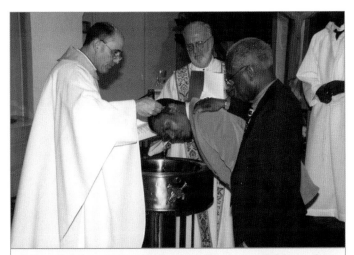

❖ *An adult baptism at Christ the King, Springfield Gardens.*

❖ *Dr. Frank Macchiarola (right), with alumni and faculty at St. Francis College.*

❖ *Bishop Daily at the 1995 St. John's University commencement exercises.*

❖ *Bishop Daily at an ecumenical prayer service at St. James Cathedral, January 2003.*

schools. A national model for Catholic school fundraising, Futures continues to make a Catholic education possible for families who could not afford one otherwise.

During the 1990's, Catholic higher education went through a process of re-evaluation. In 1991, the Board of Trustees at St. John's University approved a Mission Statement reaffirming its Catholic and Vincentian roots. The 1997 Mission Statement of Brooklyn's St. Francis College stated that the school's "Franciscan heritage and the Catholic tradition establish a cornerstone of academic excellence, social responsibility, and mutual respect." Since 1916, St. Joseph's College has contributed many outstanding graduates who have used their Catholic education to

build a more just society. At non-Catholic colleges, the Newman Apostolate has continued to provide a pastoral outreach to Catholic students.

The 1994 publication of *The Catechism of the Catholic Church* proved a landmark moment in the area of catechesis. In 1997, the Diocesan Religious Education Office organized a convocation on its use. In each of the vicariates, workshops and study days enabled teachers and catechists to become more familiar with its content and pedagogical use. Since Vatican II, the Rite of Christian Initiation (RCIA) program has become an important part of local Church life. While 208 people were registered for the RCIA program in 1982, during the Jubilee Year one thousand people were enrolled.

OUR CATHOLIC HIGH SCHOOLS:
A TRADITION OF EXCELLENCE

When the Christian Brothers opened St. James Academy in 1851, they established a tradition of excellence in secondary education that continues to the present day. Seen here are a few of the schools that carry on that tradition.

❖ *St. Agnes High School, College Point.*

❖ *Holy Cross High School, Flushing.*

❖ *Christ the King High School, Middle Village.*

❖ *Nazareth High School, East Flatbush.*

❖ *Stella Maris High School, Rockaway Beach.*

❖ *The Mary Louis Academy, Jamaica Estates.*

❖ *Fontbonne Hall Academy, Bay Ridge.*

❖ *Catherine McAuley High School, East Flatbush.*

❖ *Xaverian High School, Bay Ridge.*

Bishop Thomas V. Daily (1990-2003)

❖ *Monsignor Guy A. Massie and Rabbi Leon Klenicki.*

❖ *In the fall of 1999, Catholic Charities celebrated its centennial.*

Ecumenism and Interfaith Relations

Brooklyn has long been known as the "City of Churches," a title that has assumed a new relevance in recent years. In Brooklyn and Queens the growth of non-Catholic congregations has given a new impetus to ecumenical affairs. Approximately eighty percent of all New York Muslims live in Brooklyn and Queens, where 75 percent of the city's Mosques are located. Under Auxiliary Bishop Ignatius Catanello, the Diocese began a dialogue with the Islamic community.

A spirit of cooperation characterized Catholic-Protestant relations under Bishop Daily. In 1999, the Lutheran World Federation and the Pontifical Council for Promoting Christian Unity issued the *Joint*

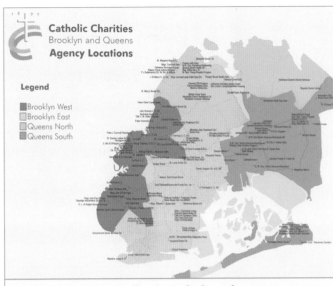

❖ *This map lists all of Catholic Charities' services throughout Brooklyn and Queens.*

Declaration on the Doctrine of Justification. At the Immaculate Conception Center, some 350 representatives from the Lutheran and Catholic communities gathered to discuss the document. In early 2003, the New York State Catholic Conference joined with other religious groups to fight the passage of a law that would force religious institutions to provide contraceptives for their employees as part of their medical coverage.

The Catholic-Jewish dialogue that began in the 1960's continued to prosper. Several local Catholic-Jewish groups have been in existence for over thirty years. The current Director of the Catholic-Jewish Relations Committee is Monsignor Guy Massie, who holds master's degrees both from the Jewish Theological Seminary and the Seminary of the Immaculate Conception. The Committee has sponsored numerous activities, including study days which help foster greater mutual understanding. During the Jubilee Year, St. Margaret's in Middle Village held a joint prayer service at which Father Leonard Badia and Rabbi Leon Klenicki offered prayers and reflections. In 2001, Father Badia was honored by a Polish Diocese for his interfaith work and named a Canon.

Catholic Charities

One area of diocesan life that transcends particular religious confessions has been the work of Catholic Charities. In September 1999,

❖ *Catholic Medical Center physicians, 1996.*

❖ *Bishop Daily at the Immaculate Conception Center with Sisters Rena Perrone, O.P., and Uche Chukwu, D.D.L.*

Catholic Charities celebrated its one-hundredth anniversary. By that time, it sponsored 180 programs in Brooklyn and Queens striving to meet the needs of a constantly changing population. Throughout the Daily years, its programs continued to be directed toward the local needs. While Project Bridge focused on the problem of teen pregnancy, SS. Joachim & Anne Nursing Home in Coney Island addressed the needs of Alzheimers patients. In a 1994 interview, Bishop Joseph M. Sullivan, the Vicar for Human Services, described Catholic Charities as a sign of the Church's unity. Ultimately, he said, its everyday work was "an expression of what it means to be Catholic."

The 1990's were significant years for the Catholic Medical Center. In 1995, the Bishop Mugavero Center for Geriatric Care opened in the Boerum Hill section of Brooklyn. In 1996, Mary Immaculate Hospital Long Term Home Healthcare Program opened. In 1999, the Catholic Medical Center merged with St. Vincent Hospital and Sisters of Charity Healthcare to form St. Vincent Catholic Medical Centers of New York," the region's largest Catholic health-care provider.

❖ *Founded in Argentina, the Servants of the Lord and Virgin of Matara are one of the newest religious communities in the Diocese.*

The Priesthood, Diaconate and Consecrated Life

The history of the Diocese of Brooklyn is a testimony to the unselfish service of countless male and female religious. While many of them continue to serve in the educational apostolate, a diversity of ministries has become the norm in religious life. Many women religious serve in parishes as pastoral associates, as Religious Education Directors, and as R.C.I.A. Directors. Others work with immigrants, in healthcare and in social service, while others work in prison ministry. Under Bishop Daily, Sister Jane Scanlon, C.N.D., was the first woman religious to become a diocesan Vice Chancellor. In 2000, Sister Angela Gannon, C.S.J.,

Bishop Thomas V. Daily (1990-2003)

❖ *Bishop Daily with the Ordination Class of 1997.*

❖ *Permanent Diaconate ordinations at St. James Cathedral-Basilica, 1998.*

❖ *A native of Brooklyn, Sister Maryann Seton Lopiccolo, S.C., was appointed Episcopal Delegate for Religious in 1998.*

was appointed Executive Director of the Pastoral Institute. Its mission includes the theological, spiritual, and pastoral formation of the laity. Over 150 years, the Dominicans, the Josephites, the Christian Brothers and the Sisters of Mercy have built up a rich tradition of service to the Church of Brooklyn and Queens.

At the same time, new communities made their presence felt in Brooklyn. In 1992, Bishop Daily entrusted St. Gabriel's parish, East New York, to the Institute of the Incarnate Word, a community of priests founded in Argentina, along with a related community of sisters. In March 1993, the contemplative branch of Mother Teresa's Missionaries of Charity opened a Brooklyn foundation. Bishop Daily saw their prayer apostolate as an important support for the Diocese's pro-life apostolate. Their new home, Queen of Hope, is in Our Lady of Victory parish. In 1996, the

Daughters of Divine Love, a religious community from Nigeria, began their ministry at St. Teresa of Avila parish in Prospect Heights.

By the time of the Diocesan Sesquicentennial, there were six hundred diocesan priests, representing 25 different nationalities. Since 1979, the number of priests in the Diocese had declined by 46 percent. In his July 2000 Pastoral Letter, *Pray the Lord of the Harvest*, Bishop Daily reaffirmed the priesthood and called on Catholic families to encourage vocations. At the Seminary of the Immaculate Conception, the formation program centers on four pillars: spiritual, academic, human, and pastoral ministry. The seminarians of the twenty-first century are filled with a love for God and a strong desire to serve God's people in the Church. They understand well the changing times and the many challenges. In their perseverance and prayerful discernment of their ecclesial vocation, they are signs of hope for the future.

Bishop Thomas V. Daily (1990-2003)

❖ *For several years, Communion and Liberation has sponsored Good Friday processions from St. James to Manhattan.*

❖ *Brooklyn Catholics attend World Youth Day, Denver, 1993.*

❖ *Bishop Daily with the Ladies Auxiliary of the Knights of St. Peter Claver at Our Lady of Charity, Weeksville, September 2001.*

By 2003, there were 165 permanent Deacons serving in a variety of ministries throughout the Diocese. While many of these worked in the business world, several have made ministry a fulltime career. In 2000, Deacon Jorge Gonzalez had directed the Hispanic Ministry Office. In 2003, Deacon Stanley Galazin succeeded Monsignor Michael J. Hardiman as Director of the Immaculate Conception Center. Other Deacons serve as teachers, school principals and Directors of Religious Education.

Since Vatican II, laypeople have sought new means of exercising their vocation while living in the world. The Secular Institutes currently operating within the Brooklyn Diocese include the Voluntas Dei Institute, the Missionaries of the Passion, the Missionaries of the Kingship of Christ, the Institute of Our Lady of Altagracia, Caritas Christi, and the Apostolic Oblates.

The Apostolic Oblates have been in the Diocese of Brooklyn since 1965, and their current chaplain is the Diocesan Chancellor, Monsignor Andrew Vaccari. In addition to their pastoral mission within the diocese, they seek to promote the international Pro-Sanctity Movement.

Third Order groups are located throughout the diocese. Lay people who join a Third Order identify themselves with a particular form of Catholic spirituality, such as the Franciscan or the Carmelite school. They enter into a period of formation and make a serious commitment to that particular religious family or tradition, whose understanding of the Gospel has profoundly shaped their personal lives.

In June 1999, a diocesan celebration of contemporary ecclesial "movements" was held at Christ the King High

❖ *This stained glass window is from St. Paul Chong Ha-Sang Chapel in Flushing.*

School in Middle Village. A day of song, presentations, personal witness, and a Mass celebrated by Bishop Catanello, affirmed the importance of these different groups in promoting the "New Evangelization." The groups present included the Apostolate for Family Consecration, the Charismatic Renewal, Communion and Liberation, the Focolare, Lamp Ministries, the National Council of Catholic Women, the Neo-Catechumenal Way, and the Pro-Sanctity Movement.

"To Welcome the Stranger": The Catholic Migration Office

In 2001, at St. James Cathedral-Basilica, the Catholic Migration Office celebrated a thirtieth anniversary Mass at which its first director, Cardinal Anthony Bevilacqua, presided. Among the concelebrants was Bishop Nicholas Di Marzio of Camden. Since its founding, the Migration Office has responded to both the spiritual and physical needs of the arriving

❖ *The Bishops gather at St. James for the Catholic Migration Office's Thirtieth Anniversary Mass, 2001.*

immigrants. Monsignor Ronald Marino, the director, aptly described its mission: "We do what we do, not because you are Catholic, but because we are Catholic." Twenty-one ethnic apostolates reach out to immigrants from some 175 nations.

215

Bishop Thomas V. Daily (1990-2003)

THE CATHOLIC MIGRATION OFFICE

❖ *Seen here is a recent Migration Office Mass at St. James Cathedral-Basilica.*

Since Bishop Mugavero founded the Migration Office in 1971, it has become a nationwide model for the pastoral care of immigrants. In recent years, as the Diocese's immigrant population has increased, it has undergone a major expansion and reorganization. The Catholic Migration Office currently provides a full range of legal services for immigrants. It helps them apply for citizenship, offers employment assistance and job training, and sponsors educational programs such as ESL. All of the major language and ethnic groups in the Diocese have been formed into apostolates, which currently include:

Apostleship of the Sea	Indonesian
Arab	Irish
Brazilian	Italian
Chinese (Brooklyn)	Korean
Chinese (Queens)	Nigerian
Croatian	Pakistani
Filipino	Polish
Ghanian	Romanian
Haitian	Russian
Indian	Vietnamese
Indian Knanaya	West Indian

Monsignor Ronald Marino, Director of the Migration Office since 1991, has articulated a central theme in the history of the Diocese. "Our particular charism as a Diocese," he says, "is to welcome the immigrant."

❖ *In 1994, Father Ronald Marino was honored by the Italian government for his work with immigrants*

Among its many tasks, the Catholic Migration Office helps immigrants apply for family Visas and offers them legal consultation. Its educational services include English as a Second Language (ESL) classes and preparation for citizenship exams. Its Resources program provides job training and placement in professional cleaning, graphic design, and the culinary arts. Perhaps better than any historian could do, Monsignor Marino has summed up the essence of the Brooklyn Catholic experience in a few short words:

> *Our charism in the Diocese of Brooklyn is to welcome the stranger. From doing so, we learn what it is to be a universal Catholic Church.*

The Immigrant Experience

Parishes throughout Brooklyn and Queens express their immigrant character in numerous ways. Each weekend Mass is celebrated in nearly thirty languages. In Crown Heights, St. Matthew's displays twenty-one flags, representing the nationalities of its parishioners. In Fort Greene's St. Lucy-St. Patrick, founded for Irish immigrants in 1843, images of St. Patrick recall the parish's Irish heritage. A statue of

Bishop Thomas V. Daily (1990-2003)

❖ *A multi-ethnic Mass sponsored by the Migration Office,* *1993.*

❖ *The Catholic Migration Office Banner is carried into St. James.*

❖ *NYPD bagpipers at the Bay Ridge St. Patrick's Day Parade,* *1997.*

St. Lucy calls to mind the Italians who came after them, while a nearby statue of Our Lady of Guadalupe marks the Mexican presence, the latest group in a parish with a long history of welcoming the immigrant. The mission of the Church is to welcome everyone, and to see a stranger in no one, thereby echoing Christ's words: "I was a stranger and you welcomed me" (Matthew 25:35). 150 years after its founding, the immigrant experience continues to be a central component in the history of the Brooklyn Diocese, then and now a Diocese of Immigrants.

❖ *Eucharistic procession at St. Paul Chong Ha-Sang,* *Flushing, June 2000.*

BLESSED MOTHER

This stained glass window is from St. Genevieve, Roxbury (1950).

EPILOGUE

"Putting Out Into the Deep":
Bishop Nicholas DiMarzio
(2003-Present)

Canon Law requires that each bishop submit his resignation to the Holy See on his 75th birthday. On September 23, 2002, therefore, Thomas V. Daily submitted his resignation as Bishop of Brooklyn to the Holy See. Ten months later, on the morning of August 1, 2003, his successor was named. Pope John Paul II appointed Bishop Nicholas DiMarzio of Camden as Bishop of Brooklyn. After he received the news, Bishop DiMarzio said that his first act was to look at the Diocese's web site (www.dioceseofbrooklyn.org) "to see what I could learn about it." The first impression that struck him, he said, was "the constant theme, 'Brooklyn, the Diocese of Immigrants.'"

The grandson of Italian immigrants, Nicholas DiMarzio was born in Newark on June 16, 1944. Growing up across the street from Sacred Heart Cathedral, he recalls that from childhood he always wanted to be a priest. After studying at St. Benedict's Preparatory School in Newark, he began his studies for the priesthood at Immaculate Conception Seminary in Darlington, New Jersey. On May 30, 1970, Archbishop Thomas A. Boland ordained him a priest of the Archdiocese of Newark.

❖ *Bishop Nicholas DiMarzio, Ph.D., D.D.*

In 1976, Father DiMarzio began his ministry to immigrants when Archbishop Peter L. Gerety appointed him Director of Refugee Resettlement. Soon he was also serving as Director of the Office of Migration. From 1985 to 1991, he worked in Washington, D.C. as Executive Director of Migration and Refugee Services

Bishop Nicholas DiMarzio (2003-Present)

❖ *Our Lady Help of Christians, Midwood (1927)*

❖ *Bishop DiMarzio celebrates the Sesquicentennial Mass at Our Lady of Perpetual Help.*

❖ *Bishop DiMarzio distributes sesquicentennial medals at Our Lady of Mount Carmel, Astoria.*

❖ *Our Lady of Guadalupe Mass, St. James, December 2003.*

to two representatives of each parish for their "outstanding service to the local community." Kevin Gatta and Father Richard Bretone, an artist and Campus Minister at Brooklyn's Pratt Institute, designed the medal.

Throughout the sesquicentennial year, there were numerous causes for celebration. In September, at Most Holy Trinity parish in Williamsburg, the Sisters of St. Dominic celebrated the 150th anniversary of their arrival in Brooklyn. In February 2004, after St.

Ann's Armenian Cathedral closed in Manhattan, Armenian Catholics moved to St. Vincent De Paul, Williamsburg. Brooklyn is now home to three Catholic Cathedrals.

On November 16, 2003, the Diocese of Brooklyn formally celebrated the Sesquicentennial Mass at Our Lady of Perpetual Help Basilica in Brooklyn. Bishop DiMarzio, the principal celebrant, called on Brooklyn Catholics to "put out into the deep together." Cardinal Anthony Bevilacqua, who had retired as Archbishop

Bishop Nicholas DiMarzio (2003-Present)

❖ *In September 2003, the Sisters of Dominic celebrated the 150th Anniversary of their arrival in Brooklyn at Most Holy Trinity, Williamsburg.*

❖ *The Most Rev. Manuel Batakian, the Apostolic Exarch for Armenian Catholics in the United States and Canada, currently resides at St. Vincent De Paul in Williamsburg.*

❖ *Cardinal Bevilacqua speaks at the Sesquicentennial celebration, November 16, 2003.*

of Philadelphia in June, preached the homily. In listing the salient characteristics of the Brooklyn Catholic experience, he identified the welcome of immigrants as an "almost signature characteristic."

Thousands of people continue to arrive from these regions through New York airports, railroad stations and highways. The Unisphere in Corona-Flushing Meadow Park and the Brooklyn Bridge can remind us of those who have settled in the neighborhoods of our Diocese of Brooklyn. As Cardinal Bevilaqua said in his homily, the heart of the Brooklyn Catholic experience is "the story of Jesus walking in this portion of His Universal Church, walking on a journey of loving and serving others."

This stained glass window is from St. Clement Pope,
South Ozone Park (1913).

ACKNOWLEDGMENTS

This book is a labor of love, a love for the experience of Church as it has been lived out in Brooklyn and Queens over the past 150 years. It is also a collaboration in the fullest sense of the word. The book you have just read would not have been possible but for the generous input of many people who gave their help and their time in countless ways.

When this project was in its final stages, we learned that Bishop Nicholas DiMarzio had been appointed our new ordinary. Right from the start, Bishop DiMarzio has supported this project, which we began at the request of Bishop Thomas V. Daily. As the diocesan sesquicentennial approached, Bishop Daily suggested that it was time for a new history of the Diocese. While all agreed that Msgr. John K. Sharp's 1954 history was irreplaceable, it was also felt that the last fifty years needed to be addressed within the context of an updated study. We hope this book has met that need.

A special thanks goes to the Chair of the Sesquicentennial Committee, Msgr. Otto L. Garcia, the Vicar General, for his patient and consistent guidance throughout the entire process.

We are also grateful to the production team at Éditions du Signe, Strasbourg, for their unfailing courtesy and professionalism. John Glover photographed many of the church buildings, schools and hospitals that you see in this book.

We are grateful to the following who reviewed the text in its pre-publication stages: Bishop Joseph M. Sullivan, Vicar for Human Services; Bishop René A. Valero, Vicar for Aging Concerns; Bishop Ignatius A. Catanello, Vicar for Clergy, Consecrated Life, and Apostolic Organizations; Monsignor Otto L. Garcia; Frank De Rosa, Director, Diocesan Office of Public Information; Very Rev. Sean G. Ogle, Episcopal Vicar, Queens North; Sister Jane Ann Scanlon, C.N.D., Vice Chancellor; Dr. Rose Zuzworsky, Assistant Director, Pastotal Institute; Ed Wilkinson, Editor, *The Tablet*. Their insights and suggestions were invaluable, as were the responses from all those who replied to our sesquicentennial questionnaire. Ed Wilkinson provided access to *The Tablet* photo files, as well as his extensive knowledge of our diocesan history. Michael Powers from the Diocesan Information Systems Office created the CD's used in the production process; thanks to Mike, the Diocesan Archives now has a digital library of historical images.

A special world of thanks must go to the following: Robert Siebel and Margaret Keaveney at Catholic Charities; John Baynes, Director, Office of Black Ministry; Msgr. Michael J. Reid, Director, Catholic Cemeteries; Thomas Flood, Director, Office of Stewardship and Development; Sister Maryann Seton Lopiccolo, S.C., Episcopal Delegate for Religious; Deacon Jorge Gonzalez, Director, Office of Hispanic Ministry; Msgr. Ronald Marino, Director, Catholic Migration Office; Msgr. Cornelius Mahoney, Director, Cluster Planning and Collaboration); Kevin M. Kearney, Attorney for the Diocese; Msgr. Martin T. Geraghty, Pastor, St. Francis De Sales, Belle Harbor; Msgr. John C. Tosi and Sister Carla Lorenz, P.B.V.M., at St. James Cathedral-Basilica; Msgr. John J. Bracken, Vicar General for Temporalities; Msgr. Andrew J. Vaccari, Chancellor. We are grateful to Tom Flood for use of the beautiful logo that adorns the head of each chapter.

The archivists and librarians encountered in the course of this project were models of efficient and courteous service. They shared our enthusiasm, provided encouragement and gave helpful advice. We are particularly grateful to Sister Edna McKeever, C.S.J., Archivist of the Sisters of St. Joseph, Brentwood; Sister Margaret Clines, O.P., Archivist of the Sisters of St. Dominic, Amityville; and Sister Rita King, S.C., Archivist of the Sisters of Charity of New York. Also helpful were the staffs at the library of the Seminary of the Immaculate Conception, Huntington, N.Y.; the Brooklyn Collection, Brooklyn Public Library; the Long Island Division, Queens Public Library; the Humanities and Social Sciences Division, New York Public Library; the Center for Migration Studies, Staten Island. A special thanks goes to Mr. Edward H. Furey, President of the Keely Society, an organization devoted to preserving the memory of America's most prolific church builder. The Brooklyn Benevolent Society provided much useful material on Cornelius Heeney.

The authors alone, of course, are responsible for any of the book's shortcomings.

Authors
Joseph W. Coen, C.A.
Patrick J. McNamara, Ph.D.
Reverend Peter I. Vaccari, S.T.L.
Official Photographer
John Glover
Spanish Translation
Deacon Ramon G. Lima K.H.S.
Graphics Editor
Patrick J. McNamara, Ph.D.

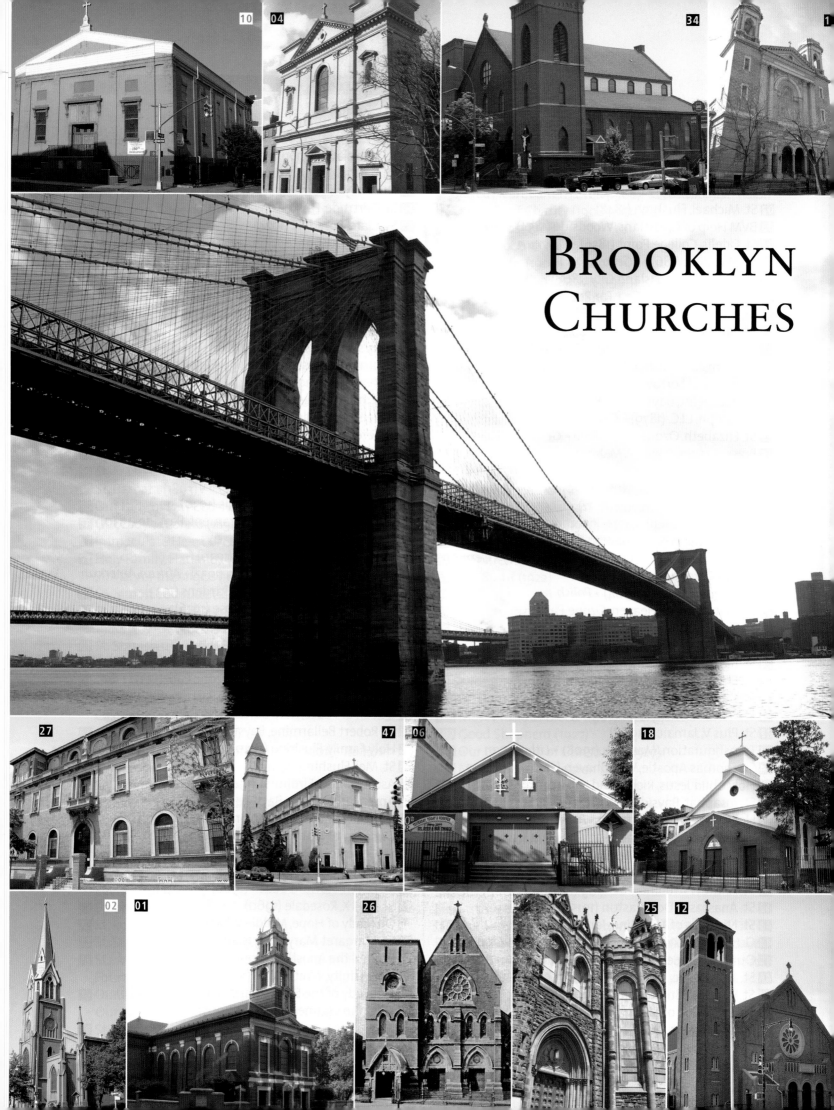

BROOKLYN CHURCHES

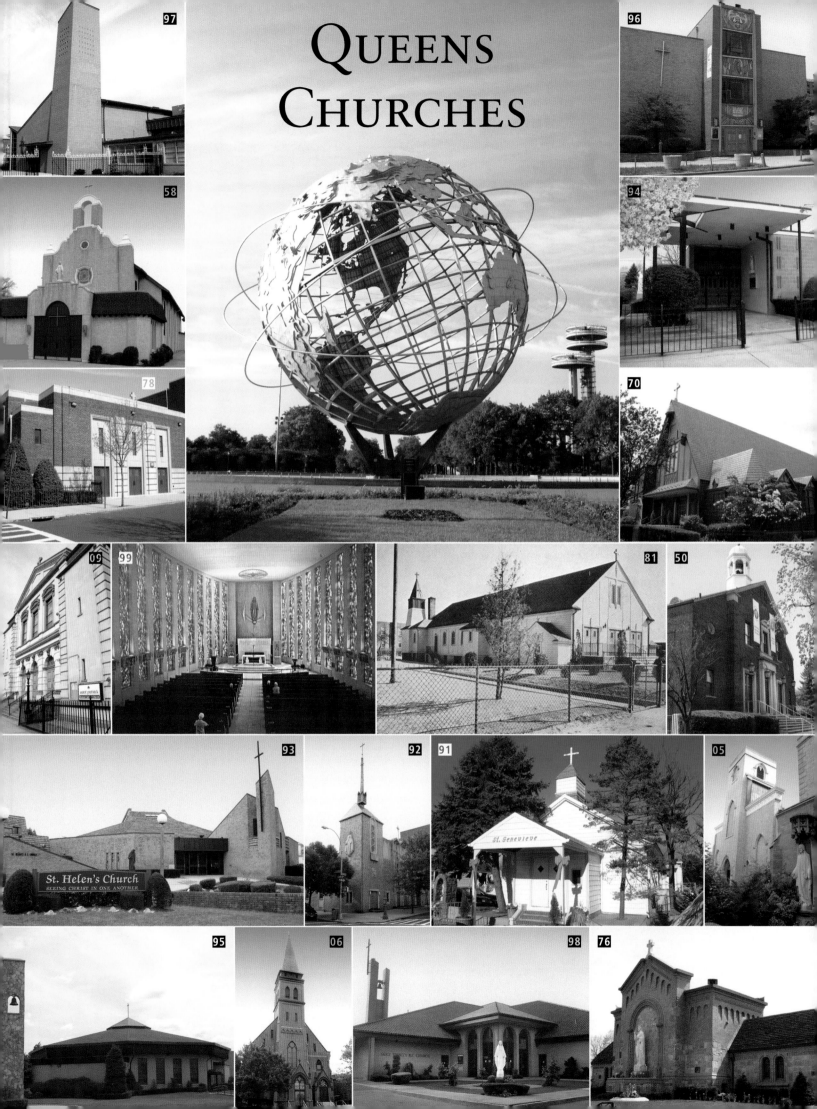

QUEENS CHURCHES

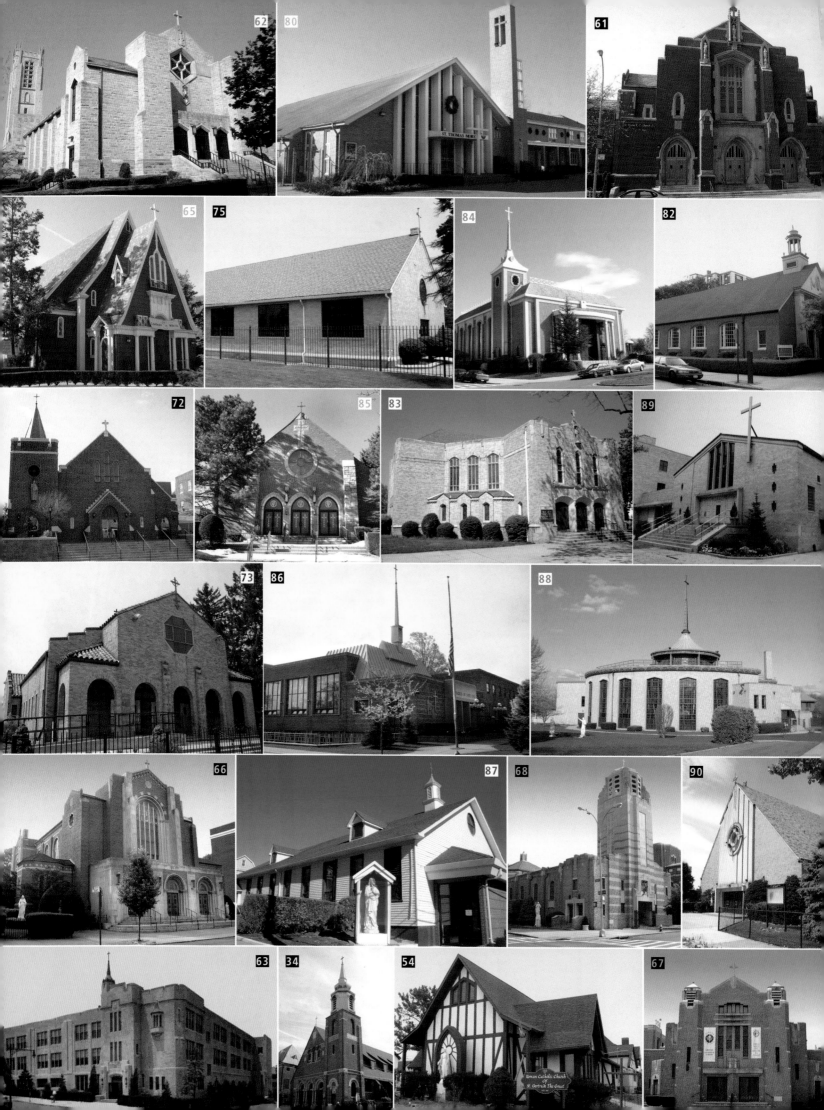